THE HEALING

Whisk

Blending Compassion and Joy into Life

By

Maria DeRosa

Acknowledgements

To my ex-husband and to my children and family—

The ones closest to you can sometimes hurt so much on their own journey that their pain becomes your heartache.

The cycle continues until you all embrace the very compass that brought you together.

Suddenly you embrace personal change in your efforts and the lessons of compassion and tolerance appear.

And now you can look at one another and say...

I love you.
Forgive me.
Thank you.
Maria

Dedication

My story-book project began with years of scribbling my whiny complaints, my anger, my joys, my fears in a journal. Once I found myself in the throws of an intense divorce, my dad battling with bone cancer and my marriage crumbling, I knew one day this book would be written and published.

I dedicate this book to all women that have that "hole" in their heart due to a loss. Pain is pain no matter how small. Therefore to all women with a hole in their heart, who seek molding themselves into a whole person once more, this book is for you.

I will roll the dough
Like my Grandmother's hands
Did before me,
Wrinkled and worn and
Fingers strong with loving -
Yes, let me fill
Wide your stomachs,
Let me stuff the pastry
With all the hopes
I have for you,
Let me bake my heart
Into every bite

By: Hannah Monsour

Contents

Chapter 1

Threshold to the Unknown

"Get out of the car!" The words were muffled through my car windows but I still understood them. I had no idea who was talking to me though. I heard the words again.

"Get out of the car!" I still didn't know what was happening, but like a good Catholic girl I listened to what I was being told. Before this moment it was a typical day like many others at this time in my life. I was ten years into my marriage, had a full schedule with teaching high school Spanish, and was raising my two children. On the way home I started feeling weird. Yes, I had been stressed but this was different. I felt completely detached from my body and trapped in it all at once. I could barely remember teaching the last three periods of the day and I had no idea where I was when the strange voice told me to get out of my car. *Am I going crazy?* I was genuinely worried I may be losing my mind, but the stress and overwhelm was so intense that I decided I had nothing to lose. I followed the voice.

I walked across the street and found myself at a strip mall on the corner of a pretty busy intersection. *I've never noticed this building*, I thought to myself as I wandered into the mostly empty parking lot. Just then, a huge sign caught my attention that read "The National Council for Alcoholism." I heard the voice again. *Go inside. Go inside now.* The voice I had heard in my car was actually my own; I was having intuitive hits and didn't realize it. *I have a few hours before I have to pick the kids up from school,* I thought, *What do I have to lose by going inside?* I entered the strange building and was met by a woman with sweet, brown eyes looking up at me from her reception desk. I felt a sense of peace wash over me when my eyes met hers.

"Come in, come in," she said, gesturing to a small couch on the opposite side of the room, "I've been waiting for you." I had no idea what she was talking about. I had never seen this woman in my life, how could she be waiting on me? But I was desperate and scared, so I took a seat on the couch and the mysterious woman joined me. The sense of peace remained and I felt safe to start talking. And once I started I couldn't stop. I unloaded on her for two hours.

"What do you remember about today?" She asked me calmly and without judgment.

"It's been like every other day," I said through tears and gasps for air, "I got up and started getting ready for the day but I noticed in the shower that clumps of hair are coming out of my head and I have this awful, painful eczema all over my hands. I know it's from stress. I've been wearing these gloves to try and ease the discomfort." I held my hands up to show her what my students had started to call my "Michael Jackson gloves" that I wore to cover the red, oozing sores. At first I thought I was allergic to chalk; a much easier thing to manage than facing everything in my life that was causing this.

"I just don't know what to do," I told her, "I don't know how to fix my life. It feels like I am doing everything wrong. No matter what I do my husband just won't stop drinking and it's ruining our lives. It's ruining the life I have worked so hard for. It's going to impact our children...I am just feeling so lost." I finally stopped talking after what felt like minutes and hours simultaneously. She never interrupted me until she knew I was finished talking. My eyes were raw from the tears, my head was pounding from the stress, and my hands were shaking because my nerves were completely shot. As I took long, deep breaths and tried to gather myself, the kind woman began to speak.

"Can you raise your head and look at me?" She was genuinely asking, not commanding. I gathered myself enough to look in her eyes and saw them filled with nothing but compassion which reminded me of my Nana when she would serve her amazing pan dulce de manzana to me after school. "You had an anxiety attack today dear, and it's not your fault. It's simply a symptom of living in the environment you have been in. Your hands look like that because of stress, and I bet you never let your mind rest. I bet your mind feels like a bunch of monkeys jumping around sometimes."

"How did you know that?" I asked amazed, "That's exactly how I would describe it."

"Sweetie, I've been there. All people who walk in these doors have. Come back and you'll see what I mean."

It was early autumn in 1986 and I had never heard of Alcoholics Anonymous. I didn't know how meetings worked, I didn't know if they could actually help me, but I knew I trusted this woman. I knew I had to learn how to navigate my own emotions and experiences caused by my husband's struggles with addiction. I didn't know it then, but this random encounter changed my life permanently. One week later I was walking into my very first Al-Anon meeting. Al-Anon is a little different from Alcoholics Anonymous or AA because Al-Anon is specifically for people living with or loving someone who is struggling with alcoholism. A few months after that first Al-Anon meeting, I thought about that woman and how much she had helped me. The holidays were approaching and I wanted to give her something extra special to show her my deep appreciation because she had offered me what many could not - the understanding of a slowly breaking heart. I bought a gorgeous bouquet from the local florist and drove down to that intersection where my life took a turn, only to find to my absolute dismay and disbelief that the office was no longer there. Not only was the office gone, but there was no sign for where they had moved, how to contact them, or where to send mail. Absolutely nothing. I was flabbergasted! Instead of just keeping the flowers for myself I figured the gesture was better than nothing so I left the gorgeous arrangement on the entry step and cried tears of gratitude as I drove home.

My husband Vince and I had been attending AA and Al-Anon meetings together for almost a year at this point and one of the very first things you learn in both programs is that the first year of sobriety is absolutely crucial for something referred to as "accepting change." No big decisions should be made during the first 365 days in the program. It is recommended that anyone who is in the program wait *at least* a year, if not longer, before making any large purchases like a home or a car, starting new relationships, or starting new professional endeavors. Vince was actually very receptive to these concepts which surprised me, but about six months into his sobriety he started talking about opening a restaurant. I made him a deal; if he could stay sober for more than a year then we could open up the conversation. I was honestly surprised by this new ambition of his; yes he could cook and he enjoyed it, but neither of us knew a thing about running a restaurant. Vince was a professional musician and music teacher, and I was a Spanish teacher but it wasn't my life's passion. I was able to open myself to the idea of co-owning the restaurant with him. He kept his end of the deal, remained sober for more than a year, kept a great relationship with his sponsor, and attended regular meetings and therapy. I was very proud of him when he came to me with a business plan and all the financials figured out. He had even found the perfect location. I was convinced that his sobriety and willingness to change equated to the level of love and respect I needed to move forward, and so we did. Picasso's Cafe was born and by 1989 we were successful restaurant owners with a staff of seven. We also offered award-winning catering services.

But with this success, our lives shifted and priorities changed. I found myself missing more and more Al-Anon meetings, and I noticed Vince was too. For years I had been starting my day with a personal prayer, followed by family time around the table over breakfast that included at least one family prayer, but eventually this natural and simple practice started to feel obligatory and we got complacent. After all, we have payroll and inventory and catering orders to worry about! No time for all that other stuff, right? The restaurant had become the first priority because it did pay our bills after all and we had employees to pay. Rationalization became one of my best friends and I had it in my head that all of my decisions were best and final. I was educated, I was bilingual, I was a teacher and a business owner, a wife, a mother - how could I *not* know what was best for myself and everyone around me?

By 2001, I was up to my ears in work and only going to one meeting a week, if that. I would skip therapy, too, and find a way to justify it. I lived on jumbo size cups of nonfat vanilla lattes. I noticed that Vince was smoking more and more cigarettes. Although I tolerated the annoying smell, it truly bothered me. I knew he was struggling with his dad's throat cancer. I saw it, I tolerated it, but honestly, I considered it quite rude that he could not take his frustration out some other way. He smoked in the office at work, at home incessantly, and never gave any consideration to me. My mom had cancer too. Neither of us were equipped to deal with the decline of our parents' health. He smoked and I bitched about the long hours to complete payroll or to cover a shift of an absent employee, and of course it all made sense as I had substantial evidence to support my nagging, scolding behavior and he had plenty of reasons to be stressed too. I didn't recognize it at the time, but with the power of hindsight I can see how much fear we were living in. Both of us were terrified of the lack of control around our parents' declining health, and even more detrimental to our relationship was the fear of sharing with one another where we felt we were falling short or what we were so scared of. I couldn't say the words out loud, but I so wanted to tell him how weak I really felt, and how aware I was that I didn't have all the answers all of the time. I wanted to tell him that I didn't always know what to do next, and that I was terrified of my decisions leading him to drink again. That terror buried deep in my heart would often take me back to days when he would come home after not telling me where he was all day. Whenever I would question him he had an easy out; he'd been hanging out with people from church or my dad, how could I be upset with him for that? And he was telling the truth about who he's been with, but all those men had complicated relationships with drinking and my intuition knew what was going on.

One day, after scheduling my mom's breast cancer surgery and finalizing the details with my dad. I went upstairs to shower. The vanity was covered with several bags from our local pharmacy. *That's strange,* I thought, *Vince isn't sick or at least hasn't mentioned anything.* I reached in the bag to find a couple of prescription bottles labeled "Vicodin" and I had no idea what that was. I decided I would ask Vince about it later and get on with my day. I had a lot of work to do at the restaurant after all.

At dinner that night it was just me and Vince. The kids were both out of the house and living their own lives at this point. *No time like the present, right?*

"Vince, I found some prescriptions today that confused me. I didn't realize you needed Vicodin for anything. Are you okay?"

"Oh, that," Vince muttered under his breath and wouldn't keep eye contact with me. Something was up and I knew it. "The dentist gave it to me for my root canal recovery, that's all." I knew he was lying. The pit in my stomach opened up to digest his lies and bury them under rationalizations and justifications. *Everything is going to be okay.* That was another lie that started to live in that house with us. Only one month later I started seeing unusual and unexpected behavior from Vince and it intensified almost daily. He would raise his voice and scream over little things. Sometimes he would simply leave the restaurant without a word and not return for a few hours later. I was grateful that the kids were long gone so they didn't have to witness all of this. Evenings usually ended in yelling and things being thrown at me; occasionally I would retaliate and throw things too. I would often lock him out of the bedroom so I could sleep, forcing him to sleep on the sofa. A spiral of high level addiction had begun. Years of sobriety were now out the door. This is what people mean when they say the disease becomes "progressive" after a long period of total abstinence.

Soon enough Vince wasn't coming to the restaurant at all and the staff, as well as myself, got used to it after long enough. It was now the new norm. The only one who kept asking me what was going on was my daughter Marissa who had started working at the restaurant for over a decade prior to all of this happening. Even though she worked alongside us for all those years after living with us for her entire life until she went to college, I was still able to hide a lot from her out of my own shame and fear of her knowing. I was so terrified of her finding out what was going on behind closed doors between me and her father. There were so many screaming matches, so many objects we had thrown at each other, so many things said that could never be taken back; I didn't want Marissa to know about any of that. I was in self-preservation mode at this point and my relationship with my daughter was and still is extremely important to me. I didn't want to taint our relationship with all the details of her father and I fighting, even if the fights were horrific and usually instigated by him.

In order to avoid conflict I simply started avoiding Vince whenever and wherever possible. He was sleeping on the couch every night and I would either retire to my room early so he wouldn't bother me or stay at work very late for the same reason. This dodge and avoid behavior was not healthy and certainly added stress to my already busy life, but it all came to a head in June of 2001 when my mom was scheduled for surgery to remove breast cancer. It had been a long day at work and I made sure that I had prepared everything necessary in my absence with the front staff; detailed notes and "to do" lists for all employees, as well as requests for friends, siblings and family members to pray for my mom. I was laser-focused on her and her recovery, trying not to worry too much about Vince or what he was doing. There was no offer from him to be with me on that day, no texts wishing my mother well in her surgery, no thought to take over for me at the restaurant. As I made the twenty-minute ride home from the restaurant that night before the surgery my mind was lost in thought about what the next day had in store, and I couldn't wait to get home and crawl in bed. The house was very quiet as I made my way inside and dropped my bags in their usual spot. I first spotted our two sweet pugs sleeping at the foot of the living room couch, and there was Vince...spread out on the sofa with countless bottles of Vicodin around him. I also spotted bottles of rum, his liquor of choice, surrounded by crushed up coke cans on the coffee table. It was like something out of a movie happening in my own living room.

A combination of shock and willingness to preserve my sanity kicked in and I felt strangely at peace. I didn't want to throw anything, I didn't want to yell or cry or blame...I wanted to walk away to focus on myself and my mom. So that's what I did. I didn't even check Vince's pulse or if he was breathing. *God, if he dies tonight give me compassion to bury him with love. My mom needs me tomorrow, God, and I do not have the strength for this right now.* I had a choice at that moment: me or Vince. I chose myself for the first time in a long time, and even though it was scary to go upstairs and get rest not knowing what I would face in the morning, I knew in my gut that it was Vince who needed to deal with it, not me. The next morning at 4:30am I walked downstairs to an empty couch and his mess was still all over the place. *Stay focused,* I reassured myself, *stop worrying where he is and what he's doing, just grab your coffee and go be with mom.* The two-and-a-half-hour drive to my parents' house was a blur and I did my best once there to be present with my mom and dad, but I felt so scatterbrained and detached from my own body. While in the hospital waiting room my phone kept buzzing and when I saw my daughter's name on the small screen I answered only to hear her in a complete panic.

"Mom, dad is driving drunk and being chased by cops! I have no idea what to do, where are you!?"

"I'm with your grandparents at the hospital, you know that. Your grandmother's surgery is today, remember?" I was trying to remain calm and collected for my daughter who was speaking between sobs and gasps for air, and for my father who was sitting directly across from me and worried about his wife.

"Mom, Dad needs us right now, you have to do something! What if he ends up in jail? You have to bail him out once they get to him and we can figure this out together, okay? We have to figure this out together!" I stepped outside of the waiting room so as not to worry my dad and to compose myself for a moment before speaking. I knew the words I was about to say would be difficult for Marissa to hear.

"Marissa, I am not bailing your father out of jail once they have him. Absolutely not."

"What!?" Her voice pierced my gut but I remained sure of my decision. "What are you talking about mom? It's *Dad* we are talking about here! You can't leave him in jail!" I heard my son, Chris, in the background and the pit in my stomach grew larger, ready to consume my entire heart. I hated having this kind of moment with my children. We were in an all-out screaming match at this point.

"Mom," Chris' deep voice cut through the high-pitched pleas from my daughter, "Marissa is right, this is *Dad* we are talking about! How can you even *think* of just leaving him there!?"

"Your father made his own decisions and for all I care he can stay there until he sees a judge. I love you both, I will talk to you later."

"But, Mom-" I heard them both trying to make valid points but I couldn't stand to listen anymore. I hung up the phone and knew that when I got home life was going to be pure hell, and I just wanted to die. *Why is this happening to me? Is it because I wasn't a good child? Maybe it's because I hit my baby sister with my purse one time when I was eight. Or maybe this is punishment for something else, but what?* The Catholic ideals I was raised on wouldn't allow detachment from responsibility in some way, even if it was completely out of my control, and I was also quick to feel guilty and ashamed. This situation was no different. The next morning I provided the money for Vince to get out of jail, but I had one non-negotiable demand: Vince was to go straight to rehabilitation and he was to go into sober living after that. He agreed to these terms and little did I know that I was at the cusp of permanent transformation. A few months after this the holidays were approaching once more and I found myself living "alone" and able to reflect on my life more than ever before. And what better time than the upcoming holidays and family anniversaries to do it?

KEY READER TAKEAWAYS

Boundaries vs. Obligations

Boundaries are restrictions you place for yourself to keep you feeling safe or to keep one from harming others. Agreements are rules we agree upon. Many of us have placed unreasonable threats, contracts and restrictions on people we love in an effort to provide safety for ourselves and others dear to us that may be affected.

What is a threat you made that you did not carry out?

Why did you not follow through?

Can you think of a time in your life when perhaps sitting down and preparing a reasonable agreement without anger might have altered a condition that was unbearable?

Chapter 2

The Weight of Holiday Cheer

My life started on Christmas Day in 1952. I was always told that I was a "special gift from the heavens" when I was growing up. Mom told me about how the hospital was short-staffed that night but still had nuns from a local convent coming by to sing to the patients and welcome the new souls into the world. She recalled to me how those nuns sounded like angels as she drifted in and out of sleep thanks to good pain medicine. At one point she was so out of it from the pain and medication that she thought the nuns were actual angels singing to her and that she had died in childbirth. Once she was back to her senses and had me in her arms I was given my name: Maria Luisa Arevalo. That very first Christmas was one I will never remember but it's one my family has never and will never forget. Christmastime became very significant in my life from day one, and as I look back on all of them, I can see so clearly now how that season was consistently one of transformation and big realizations for me.

I never had the big parties like my friends but my family always tried to comfort me by saying I was born on "the most special day" and that made me feel better when I was younger, but as I got older it was more and more difficult to deal with. I was expected to feel grateful for being born the same day as Jesus, and I somehow developed this unspoken pressure of always having to act Christlike. I came to believe that being born on Christmas presented me with a certain responsibility to behave a certain way in all of my actions. While Vince was in sober living I found myself reflecting *a lot* on what that kind of upbringing made me believe about myself and my life, as well as what my other Christmastime seasons had been like leading up to this point. In my reflections I realized my memories around the holidays were as painful in some moments as they were joyful. I came to understand that throughout my life, Christmastime was transformative, from coming into this world to learning harsh life lessons and making unforgettable memories, this time of year was meaningful in many ways to me.

It was Christmastime in 1982 and I was enjoying the holiday break allotted to me and my students. I was working at a private school at the time and even though the pay wasn't as great as one might imagine, I had worked very hard to earn respect from my peers and students. My work was bringing me so much joy around this time even though my home life and relationship with Vince was slowly deteriorating into constant verbal attacks and tension between us. I received a small bonus from the school for my efforts and decided to celebrate with the kids by baking cookies and decorating the Christmas tree, one of our favorite holiday pastimes to do together. I don't know who enjoyed this tradition more, me or them, because they loved the baking of the cookies and eating the extra dough and toppings. My heart filled with love watching them make a mess and have fun together. Once we finished decorating and eating our cookies it was time to put the rest of the decorations on the tree. Marissa was almost twelve years old at the time, and Chris was about eight. At those precious ages the wonder and magic of Christmas still overcame them easily, and I could tell they felt so proud of the tree and their work on the cookies. Just as Chris and Marissa were starting to bicker over where exactly to put the milk and cookies out for Santa, Vince walked through the door looking like the tired, worn down salesman that he was. I didn't know where he had been and I didn't really care at this point. The kids were so excited that they did not notice how much he reeked with the smell of alcohol, but I saw him drop some notes from what looked like a parish meeting at the church so I knew without even needing to smell him. Vince too was happy to see the kids and decided he would go get the ladder. Traveling back from the garage to the living room, he struggled to stand upright. We all gasped but he insisted on setting the ladder up by the tree.

"It's time for the angel tree topper, put on some Christmas music!" He slurred his words and used the ladder to hold himself up as he swayed back and forth. It happened so quickly, we were all in shock. Within the blink of an eye, instead of an angel on the tree, the eight-foot Christmas tree had fallen on him with broken ornaments as his decoration. He did not move. Our kids started crying. I looked at Marissa and tried to gather myself.

"Take your brother upstairs, get ready for bed and do not leave your room until I come in, do you understand me sweetheart?" Her sweet, innocent eyes looked back at me as she tried to understand what was going on.

"Okay, Mom," her angelic voice met my ears and I held back the tears that were stinging my eyes. Chris looked scared as he followed his sister upstairs. Fifteen minutes later, I was on the phone with the principal, my superior. Holding back my tears and mustering the most professional voice I could, I began to speak.

"I have to quit," I managed to say, gripping the receiver firmly in my hand. "Things at home require me to be here full time. Thank you for everything." I didn't even give him a chance to respond. I hung up the receiver, and left Vince on the floor. He was breathing and motionless. I dragged my feet upstairs and looked in the mirror. The woman who looked back at me in the mirror was a woman I didn't want to know or recognize. She was exhausted, living in her fear, and had no idea what to do to gain some semblance of control over her life. *You gave no notice, no detailed explanation…this is terrible. What about the bills? What are you going to do?* My mind raced as time felt like it was standing still. *Maybe if I'm home and don't have to work I can get this under control and he will stop drinking. Maybe this is for the best,* I convinced myself. I wiped away my tears and made my way to the kids' playroom, taking a deep breath with each step. As soon as Marissa and Chris saw me, their sweet voices wrapped around my heartstrings.

"Mom, is Dad okay?" they asked in complete unison. I gathered all the confidence I could muster and looked in their innocent eyes.

"He will be fine. Things are going to be just fine, and guess what? Mom is going to stay home with you more! It's going to be great. Now come on, we have one more night until Santa comes, let's get some rest." But I did not rest, and I would not truly rest for a long time after that. Things did not get better, either. Not for a long, long time.

Christmas came and went and I tried my best to pretend everything was okay, but three months later my life was centered around pinching pennies. When I was not consumed with how the utilities bills or mortgage would be paid I was in some intense fight with Vince. He was a heavy smoker and they weren't cheap. I hated them and begged him to smoke outside since we had children in the home.

"Seriously!?" I shouted at him one day after balancing the checkbook, "How dare you buy not just a pack, but a whole damn carton of cigarettes when we have loan payment due!?"

"You are just like your mom, you Latin women are always yelling and bitching about something," he said so nonchalantly as he turned to walk away from me. He knew that comment would get under my skin and unfortunately I let it. I spent the rest of the day walking around the house in complete silence, with a self-righteous look of martyrdom on my face. It was desperate and pathetic and of course it didn't work because Vince didn't care.

I was fed up and decided I was *done* pinching pennies. I had a lot to offer. I was educated, bilingual, and a lot of companies at the time were actively trying to hire more women. I was a prime candidate for corporate America. Moreover, Merritt, who was the principal at the school when I had to quit teaching, wrote a stellar recommendation letter for me, a true testament to how dedicated I was. My life unraveling had not been a complete secret from several of my coworkers or from him, and he knew there had to be something seriously wrong for me to just quit like that; it was totally out of my character. Within a few short weeks after starting to job hunt I landed a job as a bilingual worker's compensation investigator for an insurance company. Bills were getting paid, my schedule was flexible, and things were falling into place...everything except Vince's behavior. *Why can't he just get his act together?* I was constantly asking myself that question. Without realizing it, my anger was permeating all the blood veins in my body and no matter what efforts he made to apologize, my respect for him was diminishing day by day. I did not like the woman I was becoming, and I refused to see how I could possibly be doing *anything* wrong. After all, I wasn't the one drinking and causing all of the chaos in our house. I wasn't contributing to this nightmare...right?

The cycle I found myself stuck in with Vince was tumultuous and exhausting, but one part of the cycle that Vince *loved* and I mean *really loved* was apologizing. All of his apologies were over the top and they all included extravagant gifts, often in the form of flowers and jewelry. There was always a card that would simply read, "I am sorry, I love you. Vince" and each time I would allow more of my space and energy for this cycle. Even though the gifts were beautiful and shiny, I couldn't enjoy the jewelry without thinking about why it was purchased in the first place.

I was getting ready for work one day and he was not even close to getting ready. The kids had to get to school and I had to be on the road for an appointment in downtown LA . I was rushing / spinning in a total frenzy around the house.... Propelled by an underlying fuel called anger that I had become all too familiar with. He finally came upstairs to wash his face and get dressed when I pulled out my vanity drawer, completely stuffed with boxes and boxes of necklaces and earrings.

"See this! Well, I don't want it. This means nothing to me if you can't get your act together and stop drinking. And that damn cigarette smoke is not helping matters either!" I was screaming at that point and felt far from the professional woman who was getting ready to go out into the corporate world. I took out the 2x3 foot drawer, boxes and all, opened up the upstairs bathroom window and threw it all out the window. Down went all the boxes, causing jewelry to fall all over our shrubs and flowers.

"You are nuts," he said "I ain't picking any of those up!" I never did either. I was too full of pride, late for work, and had to get these kids to school. The following week, the gardeners showed up with big smiles on their faces. They were mumbling amongst themselves. I am convinced their wives and daughters were dressing up their wardrobe with what was the outcome of dramatic overreaction.

For days after the out-the-window-episode, life was quiet in our home. I was too embarrassed and self-righteous to apologize. He was desperately trying to minimize his drinking. Today I now know what they mean in Al Anon when they say, "Someone living with an alcoholic or an addict is oftentimes "sicker" without any mind altering substance." I wanted help, but was consumed with shame and fear. So we did what we did best.....ignored what had transpired and lived on with the hope that tomorrow was a new day and would be better. And it would be, right? It had to be.

KEY READER TAKEAWAYS

Looking in the Mirror

It is easy to point the finger at a loved one whose struggles with addiction have created situations or circumstances that no one ever wanted. Codependency and the mind games of "I can fix, control or somehow find a cure for this," overshadow us looking at our part.

One of the best exercises I found to deal with my inability to look at my part was this four-step Mirror Exercise by Louise Hay

Step 1

Pick a moment in your life when there was something you want to change

Step 2

Go stand in front of a big mirror alone and look into your eyes , stare into them. And say out loud: " I now realize my part in creating this condition I am not pleased with. I am NOW willing to release the pattern of behavior responsible for this condition."

Step 3

Repeat the statement in step two over and over until you believe it. (you may cry or stand there in silence)

Step 4

Take time to ponder, decide and write HOW you plan to do so.

Chapter 3

Love at First Note

I wasn't shocked that Vince would buy me nice gifts, but I was shocked that our relationship had deteriorated so much that I only received gifts when he felt guilty about something, and because of that I started to resent receiving gifts from him. But it wasn't always like this between us. Sometimes in the middle of our fights I would catch glimpses of us as a younger couple and grow slightly hopeful that we could make our way back to that version of us. The Maria that Vince met at the University of Southern California in 1971 was naive and clueless when it came to dating in the real world. I had gone to an all-girls Catholic school through all of my primary schooling, and picked USC on a whim because my father went there and I thought it was the school I "should" go to. It's no wonder that my first semester of classes was a struggle. I had no idea what to study, what I was passionate about...none of that. The only profession I had even the slightest interest in was teaching like my mom did, but I was simply going through the motions. Perhaps classes would have been easier on me had I spoken up about not knowing what I actually wanted and needed, but my first priority was making my parents happy. After all, they are to be respected. *I am to set an example for my siblings. They are paying my tuition. Wasn't this what a good Catholic child born on Christmas should do? Why should it matter what I wanted at this moment?*

I was required to take a general music class in order to complete my core classes, and I felt like a fish out of water in that class. To complicate matters, in order to pass the class I was required to critique the phrasing used in a piano sonata, and it had to be done in three weeks. The only thing I liked about this class was the professor. He spoke with the coolest French accent and wore a beret that made him almost as cute as my favorite dream boy from the latest issue of *Seventeen Magazine*. Coming from an all-girls high school, I was not used to daydreaming about my teachers, but this was college and it was different in so many ways. But I was yanked from daydreaming with this assignment announcement and started quickly scanning the room for someone who looked easy to approach so I could ask for help. I realized that the girl sitting next to me that day was the same one who had volunteered a couple of times in class and made an A on her first two assignments. *Yep, I have to become friends with her. That's the ticket.*

"Hey," I said in her general direction to see if she was even paying attention. She looked up at me and, to my delight, she had a big, welcoming smile on her face. By the end of the week after buying her lunch and giving her genuine compliments on everything from her style to her grades, I was ready to make my request.

"Amy I have a favor to ask," I said confidently one day over lunch, "Will you help me with the critique assignment? I just have no clue what I'm doing to be honest."

"Of course I'll help you!" she replied almost immediately as a wave of relief washed over my body. "Just come with me to this concert, all you have to do is sit and listen. Plus, the pianist is supposed to be a looker!" She handed me a flier and I felt a glimmer of hope that maybe I could pass this class afterall, and maybe make a friend along the way.

"Okay, thank you!" I was actually excited for the assignment now. "I'll see you there!"

Two days later, we were sitting in the dead center of the campus theater. On stage were three exchange students from the Juilliard School of Music. All I knew about that academy was it is tougher to get into Juilliard than an Ivy League school. The female clarinetist was not only dainty in appearance, her blonde hair glided over her gown like the fingers on the instrument with ease. The violinist kept looking at his audience expecting us to smile, to clap, I had no idea if that was a good or bad thing. I had never been to an intimate concert like this before and wasn't sure of the protocol. *Was I to take notes? Was I supposed to just sit and listen?* All foreign to me. Classical music was something my dad listened to in the wee hours of the night alone after we were all in bed. It was soothing. That was all I knew – this music is comfort for a tired being.

I do not recall taking any notes whatsoever that evening. When Vince began to play on the piano, I was taken to a place I had never visited. I was in paradise. The music was softer than the waves settling into an ocean bay. His fingers glided up and down the keys and he was barely touching them, yet, the music vibrated such that I was paralyzed in my skin with joyful tingles on my neck. As I listened with all my heart, I finally understood what the phrase, "I got lost in the music," meant. After the concert, Amy wanted to go backstage and congratulate the artists. She said it was a gesture of appreciation and was allowed from time to time. I felt uncomfortable as I had no idea what to say. I had not learned the correct "lingo " used by musicians. To me going backstage to shake their hands and say, "Wow that was really good, it sounded sweet," did not quite make it in my book as an intellectual compliment. So I gracefully declined.

The next day I went to my part-time job as a clerk in the stationery wing of a department store called Ivers. It paid just enough to cover my books and part of my tuition, and I enjoyed the opportunities it provided to get off of campus occasionally. That same day to my complete shock, Vince the pianist walked in the building. I couldn't believe it! I quickly scrambled to share all the details of the prior evening with my coworker as I noticed him in the adjacent men's clothing.

"Oh my god, it's *Vince*!" I muttered under my breath, "I saw him play the piano at a concert last night, he's incredible! I was glued to my seat! Oh my god, I can't believe he's *here*!" My coworker just stared at me with a look of surprise on her face too; she had never seen me like this before. Then I realized he was making his way over to the stationery looking for embossed thank you notes. I wanted so badly to tell him I had seen him play and how incredible he was but I kept our conversation to what kind of thank you notes would suit his needs best. I was far too nervous to put myself out there to this gorgeous, talented man and I barely knew anything about classical music, what could I even say? When it came time for him to pay, I knew I had to say *something*...but what?

"Great performance last night!" I blurted it out before I could catch the words and put them back in my mouth, "You had me glued to my seat!" His dark brown eyes looked into mine as he took in the compliment.

"Oh, you attend USC?"

"Yes, I'm a freshman there," I answered, feeling my cheeks get warm,

"Well I suppose you must really enjoy classical music if you attended," he declared as he pushed the store doors open and disappeared. I wasn't quite sure whether to take his comment as a compliment or not. It was time for my break. When I came back, my coworker had a smirk on her face like she had a secret.

"What's your deal?" I asked playfully," You look like you just got some really good news or something."

"Oh, nothing," she said back in an equally playful tone, "Just glad my shift is almost over." *Hmmm*, I thought, *something is up but I'm not going to worry about that right now.* My shift was almost over too and it was customary for me to go to my parents' home for dinner and family time. The two of them knew every detail of my life; how I disliked my roommate, who I was dating, how much I made weekly so I could purchase my dream car, a mustang. You name it, they knew it. But I hadn't yet told them about my run-in with the mysterious and handsome pianist. That night after work was like many others. Dad was explaining the newest feature piece in *Time Magazine*, and my mom was helping me do laundry. The phone rang and I could hear my mom say, " Vince who? Yes, Maria is here, but who are you?" *Oh my God, he called my parents' house!?* I was mortified and I knew what this meant...my mother would think I was hiding something from her and breaking one of the biggest Catholic principles...truth. Her eyes pierced me like daggers as she handed me the receiver.

"Hello?" I uttered barely above a breath.

"Hey Maria, this is Vince I met you today in Ivers, remember?" The voice was soft like the hands on the piano. I said nothing. Mom was still staring at me.

"How did you get my number?"

"Oh I went back to ask you for it, but your friend said you were upstairs in the employee room on break and she gave it to me." *Ah,* I thought, *that explains the smirk on her face.*

25

"Anyway," he continued, "would you like to go out with me tomorrow night?"

The next day, Vince pulled up in his Datsun 240 Z. He was impeccably dressed, like a model out of a men's catalog for Italian designer clothing, and he held a bouquet of flowers in one hand and a box of candy in the other. I was stunned. *Wow, this guy is too perfect.* To my surprise the candy was not for me, it was for my mom.

"Thank you for letting me take your daughter out on a date, I am sure it was a bit of a shock. However, my parents have properly educated me on how to behave. Please do not worry," he said with a big smile on his face. My mom returned the smile and off we went on our first date.

I shared the details of the night with one of my best friends; how he called my parents' house, brought my mom candy, assured my parents he would treat me well...all of it. When I was done sharing she stayed silent for a second and then blurted out a term I wasn't too familiar with.

"Red flag! He's latching on way too quickly and what's with the grand gestures? Seems a little too good to be true, don't you think?" *Oh just ignore her,* I thought, *I like the attention and it feels nice so who cares? It's not like I'm getting married to the guy, and something about this feels special.* That next Monday back in class I made a beeline to Amy. I had big life updates to share.

"Hey Amy! Thank you so much for your help with that first assignment. You'll never believe this but I went on a date with that pianist from the concert! His name is Vince and he wants to help me with the rest of my music assignments." I waited for her to process what I said.

"Okay, I get that," she said, "Just be careful, he seems like kind of a heartbreaker." I let her comment slide off of me; unfazed and unbothered were my new middle names. When I was with him I didn't have to be Maria the big sister, Maria the Christmas baby, Maria the perfect daughter, or even Maria the student. I was simply me and he was soaking it all in. I had never received this much attention from a man before and it felt amazing. As time together progressed, though, his phone calls became more frequent and I was expected to answer when he called. Otherwise he would assume I was purposefully blowing him off. During our long phone conversations he started making subtle but effective suggestions about my life. He would say things like, "Oh Maria, you can ditch that class, you're so smart that you'll still get an A. Come have lunch with me instead." Or he would say, "You're far too pretty to waste your time in that place, be with me instead." This kind of flattery was foreign to me, and it worked. I was slowly but surely pulling away from my life goals and replacing them with one thing: Vince. I started envisioning a life together; one where he would compose and perform music, maybe even win awards for it, and I would teach Spanish and live a life being serenaded by Vince. He made me believe in the romance of it all, and I thought romance was enough to make it work for the long haul.

With how quickly things were progressing with us, I met his parents only a few months into our dating, and they were not pleased with any of it. They didn't care much to meet me and were even less pleased that I may end up being their daughter-in-law. They simply tolerated my presence in their son's life and made harsh comments in front of me. They had made up their minds about me; I wasn't good enough for their son who had planned to be a professional traveling pianist recording for classical artists. I did not fit into their plan and my presence was certainly an unwelcome one. Despite Vince's best efforts to plan time for them to get to know me better it never happened. Their outright rejection of me should have been another red flag but all of the red flags disappeared whenever Vince would play the piano; I would just melt into the moment and into our love. When I would listen to him play his concertos everything else melted away; the family screaming matches and the tension between his family and myself didn't exist in those moments. I was living in my own LaLaLand built on romance and it felt like I was the star in my own movie. I ignored every single red flag in Vince and in his family because I wanted so badly to be loved and to prove I was not a failure for my choice. I wanted more than anything to show the world the girl that never did much wrong, the girl born on Christmas, has the power to make this work.

"Don't worry, Maria," Vince tried to comfort me one night over dinner, "my parents will come around, I will talk to them." He had a conversation with them that was deemed satisfactory because soon after that dinner we were engaged, and by the end of my sophomore year at USC we were married. I remember walking into our honeymoon suite on Balboa Island that his parents had graciously given to us as a wedding gift. *This was so thoughtful of them,* I thought as we approached the door to the suite, *maybe they're coming around to the idea of us.* As soon as I walked into the suite I noticed there was a bottle of champagne, chocolate, and two beds...not one big bed for us, but two beds each big enough to fit one of us comfortably. As I took in the suite and tried my best to feel grateful and not offended, I noticed a note on the mirror that read, "Ya, enjoy your evening." *Yep,* I thought, *red flag.*

Things with Vince continued to move quickly, and I was nothing but happy to be along for the ride. I never stopped to consider my own thoughts or feelings about the course our lives were taking. We decided to move to San Diego after my sophomore year at USC and I would transfer to Grossmont college. I was fine with this and never once stopped to think about if San Diego would be a good fit for me. It was spring of 1973 and I was sitting in my anthropology class. I had not heard a thing the professor had said in our one hour session, as I could only hear the grumbles of my queasy stomach. The pain magnified with each grumble. I was too embarrassed to get up from my chair because that would be disruptive and rude. Good Catholic students don't do that. Finally, the big hand of the clock was on two and class was over. I got up and ran with papers falling out of my book bag to the bathroom. Again, I threw up. Three times today. *What is wrong? Do I have an ulcer? Cancer?*

Once Vince arrived home, I explained the need to find a doctor. We were on a tight budget. After all, we were young newlyweds living in San Diego barely making ends meet to pay rent on our apartment. I was only 21 at the time and Vince was just turning 20. I found a nearby clinic that offered free services to the local college student. Vince and I seldom did things jointly these days. He was teaching part time at the college and had private students two-and-a-half hours away in the San Gabriel Valley. I was in class three full days a week and cleaned houses on the other two. So it seemed natural I would go to the clinic by myself.

The building was not only cold, with no welcoming characteristics, the room in which I was placed was bare and unwelcoming with just a few pamphlets and some medical instruments. A nurse came in, took blood work, a urine sample, and then asked me some questions. *Why did the dates of my last menstrual cycle matter? Mine had become quite erratic once we had started dating, anyway. Why did she need to know when my early morning visits to vomit in our toilet began? Dumb questions*, I thought, *this is stress. I have an ulcer.* After what seemed like hours of questioning and poking my side and insides, the nurse and doctor both came in.

"Well, Maria DeRosa, you are pregnant." The doctor's words almost echoed off the bare walls and hit me in the gut. "Not sure how far along you are at this point, but you are definitely pregnant." I walked out numb. *They must be wrong. I'm sure it is an ulcer.* I had been given nothing. No advice, no prenatal vitamins, no guidance as to what to expect or when to expect the baby. I sat on the sofa staring at the TV. President Nixon was announcing his resignation. *Wow,* I thought, *he is resigning from his presidency and I want to resign from life and hide in a hole.* I was so damn scared. All I could think of was what our parents would say. Vince was like me once I told him: numb. Neither of us blamed one another. Neither one of us were mad. We were simply numb, and had no clue what to share with whom and what to do next. The word "abortion" wasn't even in my vocabulary at this time and I knew my parents would never approve of that, so it was decided; we were having a baby.

Of course, our families were excited in their own ways but the news took them by surprise too. I was a wreck. My mom had never shared much about menstruation, let alone about birth control or pregnancy, and it was considered extremely taboo to discuss anything involving sex or intimacy at my Catholic high school. I was so sick. I thought I was going to die. I could not gain weight. It appeared that anytime I complained to the doctors of my pain it was minimized. Nurses and doctors alike agreed I was just having normal pregnancy symptoms.

All this had happened only two months after being married and moving to San Diego. Too much, and too fast. We were the topic of the secret gossip whispers among friends and family. I had to quit some of my classes to work around the pain and the constant inability to hold down food. Additionally, when we would travel to visit my parents, I would make Vince stop a minimum of two times. We knew all the correct rest stops. Neither one of us was equipped to ease the situation from numb and sad to joyous anticipation.

It was late in the pregnancy, about the sixth month, when after several visits to the doctor and countless late night screaming due to side pains it was determined I was suffering due to a severe kidney infection. I was immediately given the medication Keflex, but had no knowledge of the kind of side effects it can have on pregnant women. I was left covered in hives after just one day on the medication and I was even more miserable than before.

About six weeks prior to Marissa being born, both our parents wanted us to move back to the Glendale-La Canada area. They begged us. This really surprised us until we realized that having a newborn in a Latin or Italian family is a big big deal, especially if it's a boy. Both my dad and his dad were hoping and praying for a boy while Vince and I believed that if they wanted us home that badly it wouldn't matter.

In October, one month prior to the birth of our daughter, I remember moving furniture and wedding gifts into our new little home on Isabel Street with pride and joy. Things were slowly coming together. The pain on my side had finally subsided. Little did I know I was not helping matters by moving furniture. No one had told me that moving heavy furniture while pregnant was dangerous. The morning, Marissa was born, Vince had dressed impeccably with his newly purchased Italian shoes. He looked sharp and ready for the day. He had taken up the offer from his dad to work alongside him at the downtown furniture mart to boost our income. I went to kiss him goodbye at the front door when my water burst right on his shoes. Had I not been pregnant and had he not just lit a cigarette, I think he would have smacked me.

"What the hell is that!?" he yelled at the top of his lungs. I was in as much shock as he was. I dashed to the kitchen to wipe up his shoes and he grabbed the rag from my hands.

"Don't just stand there, call the doctor and find out what that is!"

"Ms. DeRosa, you need to tell your husband to get you to the hospital immediately, you're in labor." I slammed the phone down and felt a wave of adrenaline takeover my body. Before I knew it we were in our car and on our way to start our family. That drive to the hospital was one of total fear. We had no idea what was going on or what to expect. Since my water had broken and I was not dilating they were concerned about infection. I was in a haze from the contractions and pain levels and it felt like I was coming in and out of consciousness.

"She will have problems if we do not induce her," I heard one of the doctors say, "she has had a kidney infection recently and she isn't dilated, I'm worried about the baby." I was so confused and no one would explain what was going on. Everyone was mumbling and whispering around me and then I felt some pain where my IV was. My eyes started to feel heavy and I was so exhausted. *Damn, why did I get pregnant? Why didn't anyone prepare me? What is wrong with me? I am so dumb. I am so scared. I am going to be a mom and I have no idea what I'm doing...*And then the room went dark.

"Wake up, Maria, it's time to open your eyes now," I heard a gentle voice speaking to me but I didn't know who it was. I barely knew where I was. "Maria," the voice said once more, "you're the mother of a baby girl." I felt a bundle of blankets in my arms and opened my eyes. My vision was blurry and I was so out of it but I knew I was holding my daughter. Our daughter was the first born grandchild on both sides of the family, and even with that big title she arrived weighing barely five pounds. I didn't know I could love someone so much. She was five pounds of perfection and joy. Her name came from a famous European model and actress at the time who I just loved everything about. Vince was fine with that name, but he had to be because I made him promise to let me name our child during the countless nights of pregnancy agony; it felt only fair. I chose Gabriela as her middle name after Vince's grandmother whom I absolutely adored, and of course it helped that it was a saint name. As Vince and I filled out her birth certificate he paused.

"You know, I don't think my father is going to be happy that his name is not included anywhere in the first born child's name..."

"But your father's name is Jack...how are we going to incorporate that?" I was exhausted and getting irritated.

"What about Jacqueline?" Vince proposed, "Jacqueline Marissa Gabriela DeRosa. But we can call her Marissa."

"Fine," I agreed, "Marissa is close enough to Mary that my mother can't be upset and hopefully your dad is happy with this solution." We signed the birth certificate and on the fourth day in the hospital we were allowed to go home. For as worried and scared as I had been about becoming a mom, the moment she was in my life all the doubts washed away. She was never a burden, and instead she became my angel. I was also pleasantly surprised that our very traditional Catholic families accepted our name choices and honored our wishes to only call her Marissa. For the first time in a long time, things felt like they were falling into place.

Life proceeded fairly smoothly and normally following the birth of Marissa and through the next four years that led to me having my son Chris on Memorial Day weekend, 1978. The pregnancy with him was much easier simply because I knew what to expect this time around and had some experience. I wasn't as naive and scared anymore.

Motherhood teaches valuable lessons that are life changing and permanent. I was grateful for all of that by the time my son arrived. Plus, Chris was not a surprise. We looked at our finances, talked to our coworkers and our friends about the four-year age gap that would exist between the children, and also decided that Chris would probably be our last child. I even had time to research different birthing methods and what I thought would work best for me. I was able to train myself for this pregnancy. This time it wasn't a sprint to the finish line and I could actually enjoy being pregnant. All of the preparation made the birth so much easier this time around, and I finally felt confident about being a mom. Those children brought so many smiles to my face over the years and my heart is filled with gratitude when I think of all I have learned and how much I have grown through motherhood.

Chapter 4

For the Love of Food

Watching my children grow and learn and become their own selves opened my eyes to so much in my own life that I had never really taken the time to reflect on. Of course, neither of them were born on Christmas, so we would have the typical kids parties with goody bags and junk food and games. I loved planning and hosting these parties, but when I would be alone with my thoughts while cleaning up the house I would lament that I never had these kinds of parties when I was little. Then I would be hit with a wave of shame and guilt for feeling anything but gratitude for being born on Christmas because I was told my entire life how special it was and how it should be cherished. Not only was I born on the holiest day in my religion, but I am also the oldest of six children. This meant that I was expected to carry a lot of responsibility and that my parents had to work very, very hard to provide for all of us. This also meant they were either working nonstop or "upleveling" their skills in continuing education classes and workshops. Us children were often left with a sitter or family member until I was old enough to watch over everyone.

Food was one of the biggest question marks when trying to feed six children, so when I was old enough I started experimenting with cuisine.

One Saturday morning when I was in charge I decided to try and make French toast. To this day it is a request on Easter and big family holidays, and from the very first time I made it, I could feel my heart filling with joy and love. I realized I actually really loved serving people, and food was the first way I was able to do that. When I started making French toast for my children it reminded me so much of providing for my siblings, and I realized I have always been a provider in my own way. I learned to love and embrace this natural quality instead of pushing against it and it really helped me through my marriage and through motherhood.

Life was fairly normal for a little while following the birth of Marissa and Chris. We formed our own familian routines and traditions, and holidays were always a big occasion, especially Christmas. I would make huge meals from scratch, we would attend mass together, and of course I was always given an extra special gift for my birthday. I was teaching Spanish full-time and Vince was working as a salesman making decent money. He would lament from time to time how much he missed composing and performing music but we were parents now, we had bills to pay. We would listen to a lot of music together and sometimes even dance in the kitchen, but those times were few and far between all the other obligations and responsibilities. The first cracks in our foundation showed up that Christmas Eve night when he stumbled into our home drunk and clueless as to how his behaviors were hurting us. He had gradually started drinking more and more. First it was an extra glass of wine at dinner, and then it was a "special" cocktail after work most nights. Before I knew it Vince was in a full blown drinking addiction and I didn't have any clue how to handle it. I had children to raise and a job to work and a house to keep running. *He'll get it under control,* I would tell myself, *he's a good man at heart who is just overwhelmed right now. It will be okay.* But the longer it went on and the more I tried to convince myself that he would snap out of it, I started to lose respect and love for him. *How could he do this to me? Forget me, how could he do this to our children?* I had no tools, no resources, and no idea where to turn.

Our relationship managed to survive through the stressful moments when how much he was drinking would be very apparent. I stayed in just enough denial and he knew how to hide a lot of it from me. I was terrified of taking a long, hard look at my life and what was actually happening. After that Christmas Eve when the Christmas tree fell on top of him and terrified our children, I knew something needed to be done. Vince was in what I started calling "just-give-me-a-chance-to-fix-this mode" after that anyway. He went into what is referred to in Alcoholics Anonymous as "complacency mode" which is when the person suffering from the addiction "cares to repair" the situation. That's when the idea of owning the restaurant started to take hold of him and he made it happen by 1989. From that year until about 2001 life was good. As I mentioned in the first chapter, we had almost immediate success with our catering services and received multiple awards for our business. I, of course, quit teaching and became business partners with Vince. I still honored my Latin heritage in the food we served and Vince infused his Italian heritage into the cuisine as well. It was a hit and I thought we might actually have come out of the dark times stronger together than ever before.

But then tragedy struck. Vince's brother passed from an accidental overdose at only 40 years old, and his father was diagnosed with cancer around the same time. On top of that, a cousin who he was close with also died. All of this happened in just a year and a half and I started noticing extreme mood changes in Vince. I saw a man I didn't recognize.

He had stopped going to meetings, stopped going to therapy, stopped praying with me at our family table; he was completely checked out. So it was really no surprise to me that night I arrived home from work to find him face down on the couch surrounded by bottles of Vicodin and rum. His addiction was a ticking time bomb and our life was the target. Following his stint in sober living after his relapse in 2001, I was still too far in denial to recognize that our marriage needed to end. I was determined to make it work, especially because I was raised on the notion that divorce was a cardinal sin that was to never, ever be committed. I knew we needed to have a common goal to work toward like we did in 1989 when we opened Picasso's Cafe. So, our new marital goal became to relocate to Hawaii and in the meantime we would do the work to repair our hurt egos and damaged trust. The damaged trust was on my end, of course, and it went far deeper than I realized. Still, I was willing to try.

Vince started researching places to live in Hawaii and we decided that Maui had the most to offer us as a couple. By 2008 we had a pretty solid plan and decided to take a trip out to Maui to explore and celebrate. I was excited and feeling hopeful, but something kept nagging me once we got into our town car to go from the airport to the hotel. I noticed that Vince's phone kept ringing and he kept declining the call. He was part of our neighborhood's Homeowners' Association at this point so at first I thought maybe something had come up that they needed his attention for. *We planned this vacation for months, though, what could the HOA need that is so urgent?* I also noticed he was being very mindful of his phone, making sure it was on his person at all times and never left it on a table or counter in a room I was in. *Strange, yes, but why would he come all this way with me and make all these plans if there was anything going on?* I was back in denial mode and he was back to pretending he wasn't up to anything. It was actually the shuttle ride from the hotel back to the airport when I should have known. He answered the phone and, in a whisper, told the caller he couldn't talk but he would call later. My mind stayed in denial for another two years after that.

By the end of summer of 2010 I decided I would file for divorce. The decision was not easy and there were times I questioned my decision, but I was done fighting battles against vodka, rum, Vicodin, and other women. I was ready to live my own life and stop fighting with someone who couldn't care less about me. To my absolute shock and dismay, I found out that my children actually knew about the other woman in Vince's life. Marissa, being the first born, was always a daddy's girl and I was sure that Vince had used his Italian charm and smooth talking to convince Marissa that I was actually the one who had left him no choice but to seek something outside of the marriage. Marissa would see me working fifteen-hour days at the restaurant and how cold I could be toward her father. She saw how I let the stress get to me, so of course it wasn't a big leap for her to imagine me taking it out on her father. But she also knew about her father's struggles with addiction, so it was no surprise to her or to Chris when I called them to explain my decision to end the marriage. Although both of them were fully grown and very aware of the multitude of issues facing their father and myself, they both agreed to do their best to stay out of it and not try to mediate anything, but there were moments of tension that caused them to step into roles of mediators. Family gatherings became difficult because Vince and I were at a point where we would shoot each other mean looks or exchange very harsh words in front of others, no longer caring if people could see the flaws in our relationship. Oftentimes my mom or one of my siblings would call the next day and ask if I was okay because I had left in tears. It was a horrible time and one that caused me to reflect on what had brought us to this point. I really wanted to make sense of it all, and I slowly started putting the pieces together.

I realized just how much I had been ignoring in my own life. Vince had slowly but surely been pulling away from his sober support network including his AA group, his sponsor, his priest, and his therapist, and had instead started spending a lot of time with my dad and other church members who drank. He would assure me he had it under control but I should have known. I didn't come to full acceptance of what my life had become until I hit my breaking point and hired a private investigator to follow Vince. It felt gross and wrong but it was my only option at this point, and I needed answers. I knew at this point that our marriage could not be repaired. I would never trust him again, even if the private investigator found nothing, but of course that wasn't the case. Vince was stepping outside of our marriage and I had confirmation. It was time to start reclaiming my life.

I struggled telling people in my life about the divorce, but I especially struggled telling my dad. When I made the decision to share it with him, he told me he knew something like this was unfolding and that he loved me. My heart filled with gratitude at that moment because his opinion meant a lot to me, but he was also much older and basically bedridden by this time. He was very tired the day that I told him and didn't ask many questions, but I also think he was already very aware of why I was leaving and didn't really need to ask. He had spent a lot of time with Vince over the years and knew him well enough to know that I deserved better.

KEY READER TAKEAWAYS
Denial & Rationalization

Have you ever been so consumed with your problems that slowly you began to see no way out and rationalized the effects it was having on your body or mental state? Take a minute to write on how your reality at that time in your life became clouded.

Did you ever consciously get yourself out of the comfort zone? Did you experience a physical or emotional surrender? What happened? What was learned from that?

Start today to keep track of your emotional responses and review them weekly. This can be done simply writing out the answers to these 3 statements:

Today I was GLAD because _____

Today I was SAD because _____

Today I was MAD because _____

Notice at the end of each week is there a pattern of a person, place or thing that makes you GLAD, SAD, and MAD? Why are you allowing it?

Chapter 5

Just Me, Myself, and I

I spent eighteen months after filing for divorce driving back and forth very often between my home in San Dimas and my hometown of Glendale to comfort my mom after the passing of my dad. He died in October of 2012 prior to my divorce being final. The drive between San Dimas and Glendale was only about an hour but I usually stretched it into three or four hours. Often I stopped along the way for an Al-Anon meeting or therapy session, or simply to enjoy a cup of coffee and some alone time. I recall a particular morning on my way to Glendale, I was sitting at my usual Starbucks in Pasadena and sipping a nonfat vanilla latte, my favorite. I was lost in my thoughts as the warm sunshine beamed down on my face. *Why couldn't Vince just get it together? Why did it have to end up like this? Why couldn't he be a frequent social drinker like my dad instead of the angry, aggressive drunk that he was?* My dad and Vince were best buddies in the early years of our marriage and they were both men that I admired because of their entrepreneurial endeavors, but in my view they both drank too much, especially together. They both loved vodka but they were two different people once they were drunk. I wanted to find a man who had ambition like my dad, and sometimes like Vince, without all of the garbage that addiction could drag into life. I wanted a man who could provide for me emotionally and support me in my goals. I was open to love again, but I had no idea how or when that could happen.

Then my mind wandered to Warren. Warren was one of the regulars at Picasso's and over the 28 years that we were in business he had recommended so many people to us for dining and huge catering events. I knew that his wife had passed away a few months before my dad did, and I knew that his favorite morning drink was black coffee. *Hmm*, I thought, *I wonder if he's ever had a delicious vanilla latte like this one. I wonder what he's up to these days...*My mind kept wandering about him and I remembered one of the last times I had seen him. He came in for his usual dark roast coffee and he shared the sad news with me that his wife had passed. I remembered the look of absolute sorrow on his face, an expression of how deeply he loved his wife. I had only met her a handful of times briefly at the restaurant but I knew their love was the real deal by how they acted together. I felt the pain of losing a spouse too, even if mine was still walking the planet, and I wanted to tell him that I understood.

I found myself thinking about Warren frequently after that day sipping my latte in Pasadena but I didn't speak to anyone except my Al-Anon sponsor about it for a long time. My divorce process was still so fresh, and I honestly didn't want too many opinions from people about what I should or shouldn't be focusing on a year-and-a-half out of my marriage. But the holidays rolled around and I was spending a lot of time with one of my sisters. I decided to confide in her on Christmas Eve 2012 that I couldn't stop thinking about my sorrow, and thoughts about Warren, and I needed to get it out of my system somehow.

"Why don't you write him a letter?" she suggested. "Just put it in your journal and pretend you're writing a letter to him."

"That's not such a bad idea I guess," I said as I got up from our coffee and snacks to grab my journal.

"Just get it out of your system," she said, "I promise it will help." I followed her advice and found myself writing for almost an hour that night.

She came back over the next day to celebrate my birthday and wrap some last minute gifts. I was happy that I followed her advice but didn't want to tell her so, because then she would want to read the letter, I just knew it. And I was right. After about an hour of small talk and birthday celebration, she asked me about it. We squabbled over it for a bit but she convinced me to show her the letter. My eyes were locked on her as she read and I watched her face soften as she got toward the end of the letter. Here is just part of what it said:

Warren, I struggled for many days about writing this personal heartfelt note. I trust too, you will consider it a sincere expression. I can't begin to tell you how much I admired you and your wife as a couple. You both represented and emulated much of what I also believed marriage to be...I share all this with you for several reasons: a) I was once advised by a member of my fellowship to never pass up an opportunity to exchange kindness or offer a compliment. b) if you ever want to talk, something tells me we both understand loss and could be good friends, support and listen well to one another. Once again thank you for being such a dedicated spouse and loyal client of Picasso's Cafe. Thank you for being so gracious to allow me to share my story. I hope I did not overstep any boundaries. May God Bless you and your family, Maria.

"Maria," she said softly, her eyes filled with tears, "this is a beautiful letter. You have to send this to him!"

"Mail it to him!? Are you insane!?" I yanked the letter out of her hands but she kept insisting.

"I'm getting you an envelope and a stamp right now. If you don't mail him that letter I will! You have his address right?"

"Well yeah, I mean it's probably on one of his catering order forms, but..."

"No but's! Seriously Maria, you will regret it if you don't send it. What do you have to lose?" She gave me a very serious look but I knew her question was rhetorical, and I knew my sister well enough to know that she meant it when she said she would mail it if I didn't. Moments later we were off to the post office.

"I can't believe I am doing this," I kept saying as we got closer. I was terrified that I was about to make a complete fool of myself, but went on with life and tried not to think about it.

I was going to the restaurant less and less at this point as I was preparing to sell my half of it and make my exit. I didn't want to spend any more time around Vince than I had to and I didn't want to answer questions from customers about what was going on. We were well known in the community and it all felt too overwhelming. But with New Years coming up we were so busy with catering orders that Marissa called me and practically begged me to come in and help. I agreed, knowing all too well how stressful holiday orders could get. I told myself, *if you go simply do not interact with Vince. Don't let him push your buttons. After all, our divorce is finalized, I don't have to interact with him if I don't want to.* Was fate that on that day when I decided to break a personal boundary and go help at the restaurant that Warren decided to come in and eat? When I saw him my heart leaped into my throat. I hadn't received a response to my letter, so I decided to go up and ask him if he received it. To my surprise he had no idea what I was talking about and just gave me a funny look. I walked away in complete embarrassment and shame. *What are you thinking Maria!? The man is probably still deep in grief and you're asking him about some silly letter.* I figured that was the last time I would see him. Three weeks later my phone rang and it was Warren.

"Oh my gosh, Warren! Hi!" I sounded like a high school girl with a crush.

"Hi Maria, I am so sorry for not being able to answer you last time I saw you. I was confused and too ashamed to admit that I haven't been opening my mail since my wife passed. Thank you for your letter."

"Oh my gosh, no please don't apologize, I'm sorry for walking off like that, I was just mortified and figured I was probably bothering you."

"You're no bother to me at all," his sweet voice reassured me, "in fact, I would love to see you again soon if that's alright with you."

We went on our first date the third week of January 2013 and by the end of that summer we were already traveling together, but our third date was a complete disaster in my mind. We met for dinner at the Golden Spur in Glendora and were enjoying a nice meal and even better conversation. I thought everything was going perfectly when Warren suddenly excused himself from the table. I felt the tension enter my body and latch on. He returned several minutes later but had no idea what he was walking back to.

"Where the *hell* did you go!?" I was piercing daggers through him with my eyes. He stood in shock for a moment and just stared at me. I noticed people staring at us and I burst into tears. I was mortified and couldn't handle an audience. This was one of the first times I was triggered from the trauma of my relationship with Vince. I believed Vince was going to run out of the restaurant and never speak to me again, but instead he returned to his seat and offered me a warm half-smile as if to say, "it's okay, I'm here." When he spoke he said something even kinder.

"Maria, do you want to share with me what's going on?" His kind eyes opened up a safe space for me to share.

"I am so sorry, Warren, I don't know what came over me, please try and understand. Vince would always leave the dinner table toward the end of our marriage and he would never tell me what was going on. I came to figure out that he was answering calls from his mistress or going to the bathroom to take a pill. One time he never came back and I had to find a way home alone. It's the story I tell when I speak at Al-Anon meetings, and I am so sorry for freaking out like that. I totally understand if you never want to see me again."

"Maria," Warren took my hand that was resting by my water glass and held it up to his lips. With a soft kiss and smile he said, "I'm not going anywhere." I was so surprised and grateful that he was willing to stick around. But my outburst showed me that I needed to keep working on my end of things. I needed to release my anger and I needed to find ways to alleviate stress. I started running, attended more Al-Anon meetings as both an attendee and a speaker, and added extra therapy sessions as needed. I was slowly healing and my relationship with Warren started to blossom.

Warren was slated to play maxi-basketball at the Senior Olympics in Europe that summer and asked if I would want to come with him; of course I said yes! Not only did I love watching basketball, but the games were in Italy! How perfect! Warren handled all of the details and travel arrangements, and I was so grateful that I wanted to do something to return the favor once we were in Pompeii. I hired a personal tour guide to take us around Pompeii and it was an amazing experience. She took us into the more popular spots and some hidden ones too. Toward the end of our tour, in the middle of a ruined area where plays and town halls used to happen, she told us that there was a certain spot where you could be heard in all four corners if you sang loud enough. There was a huge tourist crowd coming up behind us so I knew if I wanted to try it out this was my chance. I wanted Warren to see my courage and willingness to go out of my comfort zone. Trust me, I'm no opera singer, not even close, but I decided to sing two verses from a Spanish birthday song that my Nana used to sing to me. When I was done, to my complete surprise, I received a huge round of applause and Warren had filmed it all. I stood for a moment taking it all in and I was so proud of myself. Then, like something out of an Italian romance film, Warren walked up to me, kissed me on the forehead, and said, "Maria, you make my heart sing in more ways than one." I melted into the moment and knew that I had just found my heart in Pompeii.

In 2014, about a year after our trip to Italy, Warren and I decided to move in together. This was a huge test of trust for me. Yet this man was so gentle and wise, I just couldn't imagine him hurting or betraying me. We had fun together and he was so sure of himself and what he wanted out of life, and I was a huge part of what he wanted. I felt truly loved for the first time in a long time. One day as I was moved in and busy with unpacking and laundry and all the things, Warren came up to me and took my hand.

"Can you come with me?" his kind eyes looked into mine.

"Right now?" I asked with a smile.

"Yes, my love, right now."

Even though I was busy and wanted to get the house in order, I couldn't resist time with him. I dropped the laundry and before I knew it, we were flying over the San Gabriel mountains in a private helicopter. I was so grateful that I left the laundry behind. And I was so grateful I had left my old life behind. In that helicopter, holding Warren's hand and looking down at where we lived in awe, I couldn't help but think how differently life could have been had I not set boundaries for myself and broken the cycle that Vince and I were stuck in. How could I set boundaries for myself with Vince when I didn't even know what a boundary was? I was only 19 at the time and I couldn't hold that part against myself, but there was a lot that I did feel responsible for and it was time to reflect and heal that part of me.

When the helicopter landed I couldn't stop thanking Warren for such a beautiful afternoon. He could tell how much I meant it but I could also see that something was on his mind. He asked if I wanted to grab a bite at one of our favorite restaurants and of course I agreed. Over dinner I could tell he wanted to ask me something, but I wanted to give him the space and time he needed to ask it.

"You looked so deep in thought while we were up there," Warren said, "What were you thinking about?" He wasn't asking it in an accusatory tone the way Vince may have. He genuinely wanted to know, and I genuinely wanted to tell him.

"I was thinking about all of the crazy places life has taken me that have been total surprises. Like today's adventure. I've done a lot of unexpected things and I was just thinking about...well about my life I guess."

"Ah, okay, that makes sense. Anything you feel inspired to share with me?"

"I'm just honestly kind of amazed at how far my life has come since that very first Al Anon meeting. Did I ever tell you about that?" Warren shook his head side to side and kept his eyes locked on me, waiting for me to speak again.

"God, what a time...Vince had found some pamphlets for Al-Anon on our couch and he was really annoyed about it. All I could think about was that I didn't want to have anxiety attacks anymore and that eventually our kids were going to start noticing his behavior. My stomach was always in knots and I didn't know where to turn. So I told Vince I was considering going to meetings and thankfully his only reaction was to go outside and chainsmoke instead of throwing anything or yelling at me." I paused for a moment to gather my thoughts and Warren didn't speak. He was giving me all the space for this moment. "I knew I couldn't let it be known that I was going to meetings so I started making excuses to get out of the house and Vince was too wrapped up in his addiction to really care or ask where I was going. Well, I showed up at my first meeting feeling hopeful and ready to start making some changes and it was awful."

"Why was it awful?" Warren's familiar look of concern washed over his face. He was such a kind man.

"I walked into a room with much older women who had all clearly been attending meetings together for ages. They all seemed so happy, and I was clearly not. They each brought their own lunch and had their "usual" chairs to sit in and I just felt like a complete outsider. Of course, I stayed at the meeting because I was desperate but I felt completely alone in that room full of women. I didn't want to give up so I found another meeting and then another and another before I found the people that felt right and safe for me. But that's the thing - it was so hard for me to feel safe to share without judgment. There was just so much happening behind closed doors..." My thoughts trailed off for a moment as I took a sip of water and some deep breaths. Warren was focused and not pushing me to say more than I was ready to. "Once I finally started sharing stuff in Al-Anon I realized how much shame and guilt I was living in. I had lived on a merry-go-round of addiction for years and years and instead of trying to do something about it sooner, I just focused on how to make life *look* like it was okay, even if it didn't actually feel okay. Vince hadn't placed me there on purpose, we were both trying to get off the merry-go-round and just couldn't. And today, on that helicopter with you, for the first time in a long, long time, I feel like I am finally off of that merry-go-round."

"Maria," Warren said after we shared a few moments of silence, "I love you. Thank you for sharing that with me."

"I love you too, Warren, thank you for accepting me as is." And from that moment forward I knew I could tell Warren anything and that he would never push me to share before I was ready. I had never felt so safe talking about how I felt or what I thought, and a new level of love was unlocked that felt like a warm blanket wrapping around my heart.

KEY READER TAKEAWAYS

Intuition & Confidence

Have you ever taken a bold step or action you thought was just impossible to do?

My sister prompted me to do the very thing I was avoiding.

Try this exercise: Ask Your Intuition A Question

Write out a question, a concern, a feeling that keeps popping up and then sit with it. Take time to ponder it.

1. Do any answers seem to arrive in your mind ?

2. Journal about anything that comes up that could be a potential answer or piece of guidance. It may take time. Maybe nothing does. Do NOT get discouraged

3. Focusing on the question at all is enough to bring you an answer when the time is right. Sometimes it will be a person, place or thing that is totally unrelated. Just dare yourself to try.

Chapter 6

Rolling Life into a New Dough

One of the things I loved most about life with Warren was how easily he could make me feel special, and not with extravagant gifts only like Vince. Warren really cared about how I was feeling, and what I wanted out of life. He encouraged me in all aspects of my life to go after what mattered to me and what made me happy. In 2016, for example, when I signed up for a 10K at the Senior Olympics in Utah, Warren cheered me on the whole way. I was filled with self-doubt even though I had earned my qualifying place in the race, and when the race started I was totally stuck in my head. Within one minute of the race starting I took a hard tumble onto some uneven gravel, and the old me would have taken that as a sign to stop; but that was the old me. I had trained and prepared for this race for months with Warren's encouragement and I heard his voice in my mind combined with my own, and both were reminding me not to quit. *Get up, Maria,* I heard the familiar voices say in unison, *don't let this fall make you quit! Just get up and run like hell, you can do this!* My hands were bleeding and my right side was in pain but I persevered and finished that race. Not only did I finish the race, I placed ninth in my age category with over thirty runners in my group! After that I had more confidence than ever and I decided to start training for a whole marathon.

I decided I would run the Los Angeles Marathon in 2017, and I did it! I completed it in under five hours, too, at sixty-four-years young. I was so damn proud of myself and was starting to feel my integrity and power again.

I had not felt *that* confident and *that* sure of myself since I broke off the marriage with Vince and started living on my own in 2010, but I was also dealing with a lot of heartache and pain at that time. It was such a freeing and simultaneously confusing period of my life. The house had never been as quiet as it was once Vince moved out, and the silence pushed me to find ways to occupy my time. I didn't really know what being single was going to mean for me, but I knew I was determined to forge my own path forward one step at a time, just like when I was running that marathon...one foot in front of the other. Being single was freeing and exciting at first, but then it became monotonous and almost depressing. While I felt free from the old obligations that were holding me back, I also had no idea how to live life without all of that. Who was I if I wasn't the wife trying to save her marriage, the business owner trying to juggle it all, and the mom who had to tend to her children? Who is Maria? I was determined to figure it out.

This is where my Al-Anon group, my sponsor, and my therapist deserve all the credit in the world. If there was one thing they had taught me that had stuck with me through the divorce process it was: let it begin with me. This idea then evolved into: I do things for me and only me. In other words, if I give my energy to something that is important to me, no one has to know, validate, applaud or notice it. It was extremely difficult at first, especially because my dad was dying and I was driving to Glendale almost daily to see him. But little by little I started doing stuff for myself. It started with solo walks and runs, and then I started treating myself to self-help books to read with my morning coffee.

There were moments when I would feel selfish for enjoying myself, and I would tell myself to focus more on the future, but I also knew I deserved this time to figure things out and relax a little bit.

At the suggestion of a close friend I started attending a class all about grief and separation, and I had no excuse not to go; the class was free. It was here that I realized my sadness and lack of willingness to practice any self-care was a natural state of grief. I was grieving the loss of my 38 year marriage, my 28 year restaurant business, and to top it all off my dad was slowly withering away with bone cancer. It was all just too much and no one would have blamed me for giving up, but something deep down in my gut kept me going. I was free from the chains of all that attempted to control in my life. I had attempted to control my husband's drug abuse and behavior. I would go to work and oftentimes reprimand my employees for little things –like forgetting part of their uniform, just so I could scold. I would tell my mom to go for a drive, to let me be with dad, and to not worry. I was the eldest daughter, I could handle it. All this so I could feel safe. Being in control, receiving accolades, being a good Catholic girl...all of it would somehow provide love and make me feel safe.

A few years into my healing journey, January of 2013, I made my very first vision board. Feeling inspired by the many books I had read about self-love and following your own path, I set out to start picturing my new life; something I had been terrified to do up until this point. I bought a bunch of magazines including *Cosmopolitan, Women's Magazine, Runner's World,* and *Glamour.* One of the first articles I stumbled upon was in *Cosmopolitan* and the title read, "I Will Survive Divorce." I grabbed the scissors and cut carefully around the letters. It went at the very top of the vision board. I spent the rest of the afternoon cutting out words and pictures that made me feel safe, confident, happy, and excited to take on this new chapter in my life. Just one week after I made that vision board, Warren and I started dating. It was during an Al-Anon meeting around the time I started dating him and I was sharing with my group that I had met someone. One of the older women in my group came up to me after the meeting and asked if we could talk.

"Of course," I said, "What is it?"

"Well I know this may sound rude, but I am not trying to be. How did you find such a good man? Was it getting your confidence back that made it happen?" Her question caught the attention of another woman standing nearby and she joined in on the conversation. We stood there and talked for almost an hour while I answered all of their questions about how I walked away from such a long marriage and the finances that were part of it, and about why I didn't fight more for what I was entitled to in the divorce. I often asked myself these questions but the answer always came back to one thing: I did it for my own serenity and nothing else. Seeing these women so intrigued about my journey and wanting pieces of advice from me really inspired me to keep going to meetings and showing up for no one else except for myself.

To practice showing up for myself, I started picking one thing to do each day that was new, and one day I woke up and thought, *I should go to the salon and get my hair dyed and just let the stylist pick what we are doing. That could be fun!* I was trying to make "fun" my middle name during this second chapter of life, so I did just that. I walked into my regular salon, told my hairdresser what I wanted to do, and told her to surprise me. And surprise me she did! The chair spun around to face the mirror when she was finished and I had gorgeous purple highlights in my gray hair. And I *loved* them! I could *not* stop smiling that day and I still have shades of purple in my hair to this day. It's amazing what just choosing something for yourself can do to heal the spirit.

Shortly after my mini makeover, I found out I was going to be a grandmother! It was almost exactly a year out from my divorce and I was in such a beautiful place in life to be able to give and receive the kind of love that comes with a new child. I went into teacher mode and created a plan, and the plan was built around my daughter-in-law going back to work after healing. I believed I would be splitting babysitting duties between me and her mother. I got to work right away, turning the bonus room in my house into a playroom complete with a rocker, a crib, stuffed animals, clothes, and plenty of toys. I was so excited to welcome a new bundle of joy. However, once Bella arrived into the world we all were surprised at how our roles changed. Grace, my daughter-in-law, craved to be a stay at home mom and became fiercely protective over her child which I completely understood. I didn't get as much time with Bella as I had originally planned but I was used to things not going to plan at this point and I wanted my son and his new family to be comfortable. But these changes happened very quickly and even though I was becoming more flexible with time, my need for structure and stability overlapped with my emotions, which mixed with all the hurt and pain still left over from the divorce. This mixed pot of emotions, along with everyone attempting to understand their new roles in parenthood and in the family, altered us. We all developed new personalities. There were multiple moments of rage, fights and not-so-civil-text-messages. I know I am not proud of some of the things I said or how it added to the tense situation at times, however, today I can say I am at peace. Furthermore, with confidence, I can also say that we enjoy a special family unity, now. We are at peace. We enjoy one another. All because in time, we realized each of us was required to heal.

I sat down after several months of analyzing and bitching in therapy, after sharing and crying in the rooms of Al-Anon, and after countless nights of whining to Warren. I sat down and wrote this poem in 2017 to get it all out.

"NANA? GRANDMA? GRANDMOTHER? WHO AM I TO BE?"
Grandmother has a name, a face, a special place in my heart
Yet the universe & several others joined hands to uncover my part

You see in my mind I had a vision, a dream on how being a
grandmother would be
But God and the universe in 2014 had additional lessons for me.

Is not a grandmother to babysit? Yes babysit, read stories with
grandchild?
Or was I to watch from afar simply to be quiet, meek and mild?

I wish there had been a manual on how to interact with son, baby and
wife
What was I doing wrong? Not realizing they had their own strife.
My eyes were hidden to any of their family tension behind a closed door

Often I thought, am I only good for running an errand to the store?

In time I came to see it was not my place to judge, it was not me.
It was about past circumstances in life. "Maria, simply accept and just BE"

I had a hard time at first feeling so rejected, unloved and alone
Until all those that loved me said "enjoy time- moments...don't groan"

It is not easy for me to change my outlook, sit back and comply
My M.O. is to analyze, to ask WHY? Oooh brother, why??

Time has passed and now I truly see...
life is not always how I feel, it MUST BE.

I tell myself: would you rather show up bitter or in a state of total
"gentle-still"?
You have the power to shape special memories and yes in time, you will.

THE HEALING WHISK

Today my granddaughter is 9, and I can recall lots of hiding-games galore
What An awesome story teller she is and so much more

Glad I did not force and expand on my expectations & create drama
Then I would have added terrible sickness to the heart trauma

I am not pizza, not everyone will like what I offer or who I am
But I have the power to leave each family member with a blissful bam!

And so I have come to find
Blood connection does not define

The stories, beliefs and judgments we develop each season of life
Can bring us joy or cause us extreme strife

Some experiences foster uncertainty, fear and often pain
However, being flexible and willing, grants us many gifts to gain.

Yes, the road of grandmother was nothing how I anticipated it would be
But it has brought son, granddaughter and wife in a special bond of 3

The benefit to me? (or so I see)
Jointly, our family grew from afar
I now have countless notes, pictures and texts with a star.

You see it is easy to blame and point the finger to another for your pain
you gain little but severe emotional, deep strain.

When my life transitioned from single woman, divorced, & soon -to-be-grandma
I trusted life would be continuous moments of "hurrah- hurrah!"

Holding onto "Come on we can make this happen!" PLEASE!
only leads to the road of sadness, grief, little or NO ease.

It took some time for me to accept , to allow time for healing, to let life unfold

NOW, and forever, my granddaughter's sweet hug, I treasure and hold.

And so it is.
Carpe Diem

And so it was indeed. By 2018 Warren and I realized that our plans in California weren't panning out the way we had hoped. We realized that after almost five years together our second chapter in both of our lives, and the plans that we had carefully woven together, were unraveling at the seams. I had visions of being a part-time babysitting grandmother and restaurant consultant and Warren had visions of possible coaching at a nearby school. In both of our families we noticed that dynamics were changing and our vision did not fit. My daughter-in-law chose to be a stay at home mom and Warren's basketball connections and team were dissolving. We both decided that a geographic move to a desert community would provide us with a fresh start. We could start our second chapter away from both our past lives in San Gabriel Valley. It was necessary not to be so close to the places and memories that reminded us of our past every day. The desert, Rancho Mirage specifically, was perfect. It was only a 2 hour drive away from those we loved and an environment with new faces, landscapes, and activities that were completely opposite from what had been familiar to us.

Once there though, I couldn't get to a place where I felt grounded enough in myself or confident enough to seek solutions to my finances, or to start planning what my life leading up to retirement would be like. I found myself running the streets of Rancho Mirage daily, huffing and puffing, hoping for direction with the desert breezes. I needed the badge of a "newly divorced woman" to be replaced with something of my own. While in the midst of indecision, I took up pickleball and aerobic classes sure to spark friendships that might enlighten me. Should I return to the teaching field? What about being a concierge in a local hotel or part time hostess at one of the high end restaurants? No, I was done with both. Yet, I knew I loved bits and pieces of what I could do. Furthermore, I was really good at it. I wanted to participate in my own recovery, but how? I sought out guidance whenever and wherever possible. I knew I had to rely on experts. It was not easy for me to ask for help; after all I had been the teacher. People came to me. Additionally, seeking out help often required a financial investment as well. However, as a former teacher I knew one thing: knowledge thrives when the material is presented with fun, consistency, and with a person that communicates it all with love.

Fast forward a few years, Warren and I were living at peace and happily in Rancho Mirage and I was enjoying getting my new business off the ground. Coming from owning a brick and mortar location for almost 30 years, there were so many things I had learned about business. One of the things that used to give me the most anxiety was the dreaded employee payroll, and not because I didn't want to pay my employees, but because as a co-owner I was always running numbers in my head and saving a dollar wherever I could. Usually Vince and I got paid last and sometimes we didn't pay ourselves at all. Meals for the kids were often leftovers from the day at the cafe. It was scary. Sleepless nights were customary. Yet, we were determined to make it work.

I had an advantage in starting my newfound business, Ladies of the Kitchen. I had some collateral and a small financial investment I could bring to the table. What I lacked was confidence and tenacity. I had 28 years of cooking and baking under my belt. I had 11 years of teaching others Spanish and writing skills. But none of that mattered if I did not have the belief that I could create a platform, and I did not believe it. I had to change my mindset. It took lots of journaling, reading, and reflecting to see that my intention needed to shift from making money to add to my own security into enjoying money and all the things it could bring into my life. Money could be magical and not just stressful!

And I came to see that a shift in mindset to make money fun again (I know, sounds crazy, right?) that more actually flows in. To me that sounded so corny at first. Like wishing on a genie bottle. I wanted to replace the financial security and safety I was used to and I wanted it all back fast. I did not want to depend on family or Warren for help. Furthermore, I was oblivious to all the goodness around me because all I could focus on was making more money. And I learned another lesson quickly during this time: when you're willing to ask for help and surrender to receiving it, help arrives.

KEY READER TAKEAWAYS

Learning to Trust Again

I give credit to one of my mentors, Tracy Litt, for this simple exercise. Each weekend I take time for what I call: Reflection and Celebration which is quiet time alone with pen, paper & maybe a candle or crystal you love. Here are the journal prompts to go through each time you do this:

What action/behavior makes me feel good about this past week?

Was there a situation this past week I could have handled better

Did I give in too easily by saying YES to something whenI should have said no?

How will I go about planning the week ahead so that I make time for me, my spouse/partner and a friend or family member?

How did I celebrate my wins? What excites me about the week ahead?

Chapter 7

Is Change Possible?

I started Ladies of the Kitchen not really knowing what it would transform into. I knew I had a passion for cooking, teaching, and helping people. Surely I could combine all of that into something profitable, right? I knew I loved the work I was doing with coaches and mentors, and I thought maybe I could step into that role for someone or maybe multiple people. I was open to whatever the Universe had in store for me and I followed my gut, unapologetically, for the first time ever. I knew I needed to start small so I didn't get overwhelmed, and I wanted it to feel completely inspired. I knew I wouldn't stick with it if I didn't feel its purpose in my soul. I read an interview in a magazine with Oprah Winfrey and she said that when she was a girl she would lay on her back and stare at the clouds for hours. Some of her biggest ideas would come to her when she did that, so I started there. I pulled out my favorite blanket that my sponsor had knitted by hand for me, went into my yard, and I looked up at the sky. I heard a voice with the swallows passing overhead and the rustle of the bougainvilleas. "Just be a kid again. Do what you love." Dreaming transitioned into mindful meditations and I let myself breathe into my dreams. And the best part about it was that I knew it didn't have to be perfect.

I took what I loved, dancing and baking and sharing inspiration with others, and started a YouTube channel. I had no idea what I was doing and sometimes I wouldn't even hit upload on some of the videos I recorded, but I was trying and that was all that mattered. Warren was so supportive through the whole process of me trying to figure it all out. I would set up the lights, the tripod, and the camera, and stumble my way through trying to make good content for my brand new, and unknown, audience, and Warren would be there cheering me on. Even if I didn't upload the video, he would encourage me to keep going, don't give up. Slowly with his encouragement, my weekly and monthly commitments to coaching and learning new tools , my confidence returned. I started to experiment with balancing my work calendar with sport and family activities. And then the vision and my mission started to bloom. And the key seemed simple enough but it took time to understand what it was - love. I loved what I was trying to make happen, and most of all, I loved myself enough to try. I started putting mantras on Post-its all over the house that said things like, "I am the master of culinary ideas in the kitchen," "I help and heal others with food," "I am a teacher of health and wellness," and "I use therapy in the kitchen for all 5 senses." Slowly I started to believe what was written on them and anytime I started doubting myself I would find one of those Post-its and read it to myself outloud three times in a row. My life had turned into an adventure; one where I was free to explore and learn and share what I was learning with others who were open to hearing it. I had finally left the role of teacher and embraced being a student of life!

As I started gaining more and more confidence in myself and the knowledge I had acquired over my almost three decades as a business owner, the "lack" mindset I found myself stuck in so many times seemed to melt away. Of course I still had my off days where things didn't feel so easy, but everyone goes through that, and I knew I didn't have to do everything perfectly anymore. That relief of pressure on myself opened me up to so many possibilities and opportunities to learn from myself and from others. I started leaning into the fun part of filming videos and stopped worrying about them being set up perfectly and speaking properly all the time. If I slipped up, it was okay. It didn't define me. In fact, some of my *best* moments interacting with my audience came from me laughing at my own mistakes and showing them it was okay to do the same in their own lives. I quoted Julia Child a lot in my videos with her iconic line, "Well I guess the recipe is toast!" And when I leave this Earth and enter whatever is in store next, I hope I can say that I used every last ounce of my innate talent that I was given at birth to help people and make a difference. I can die happy if I complete that mission.

One of the most impactful books I read during the time I was starting my business was Tracy Litt's book *Worthy Human: You Are the Problem and the Solution.* I chose it to read based on the title alone. *How can I be the problem and the solution? That doesn't even make sense...* But it would make sense soon. I knew I was part of the problem in Vince and I's relationship from the first Al-Anon meeting I attended, but how could I also be the solution? I was ready to learn. I read that book cover to cover in only a few days and it truly changed me. I knew I needed to absorb much more from Tracy Litt and I wanted to dive head first into her pool of knowledge. I scheduled a discovery call with her and held my breath in anticipation. I just had a feeling about this woman. She was going to understand me and she was going to help me. And I was right.

My very first call with her lit my soul on fire. *Finally, a woman who lives the luxurious life I want to live but is still so grounded in herself. And damn she can talk.* Tracy was a TEDx speaker which I really admired but even just in conversation Tracy would say prolific things so casually, as if it was coming to her as easily as breathing. I felt seen and understood by her, and I decided I needed to join her at her Worthy Human Live retreat in 2020 and continue one-on-one coaching with her. I needed to take my healing further because even though life with Warren was going so smoothly, I was stuck in my fears. *This just seems too good to be true,* I would tell myself, *and what if he's hiding something? And even if he's not, do I even deserve this? What if our bubble of love pops and I'm left heartbroken again?* So, so many what-ifs and I was desperate for reassurance or some kind of sign from the Universe. I had to willingly open myself up to answers, even if I was scared to receive them, but once I did open myself up I actually felt more confident than ever! The message I was receiving from the Universe was that this was *my* time, finally! It was my time to reach for the highest mental, spiritual, and physical healing possible. I knew it would take time but I also knew I could do it.

Once I found the perfect combination of working with Tracy, going to therapy, attending Al-Anon meetings, working for myself, and leaning into my love with Warren, I realized I had put all the pieces in place to create a really good life. I was slowly knocking down the building blocks I had placed carefully in my past and was willing to choose new blocks. That was huge for my healing. I was learning to be fun, discover what I enjoyed and share the good, the bad and the ugly. I was not perfect and that imperfection was how others related to me. Together we understood pain, and soon, through sharing and deep conversations, we started to see there was hope for us all. I slowly chipped away at the layers of beliefs and habits that were no longer of benefit. I would still get triggered from time to time, which is totally normal, but instead of trying to fight the tears and shove the feelings down I was learning to embrace and process it all. I was starting to understand myself, for the first time in maybe my entire life, and I realized there could be so many other women out there who need to do this kind of work. I wanted to help women like me who were starting a second chapter in life, or a third, or fourth, and just wanted to connect with themselves and their purpose.

As someone who started over at 58-years young, I knew the kind of societal pressures and norms that most women my age faced, and still face to this day. There is pressure, especially on older women, to be educated, raise a family and stay head of that family, and on top of it all, maintain a good paying job that sets you up for retirement. I realized with so many women I started working with that there was this major resistance to accepting their own flaws. To admit any type of character defect was just not part of our feminine make-up. It was tough to admit that change had to start internally first and then externally. I always found empathy with these women because I had been there and knew that mindset all too well. I would tell them all the same thing: if you're open to it, I would love to teach you about radical personal responsibility. Usually their ears would perk up at this term, and I would go on to explain that once you can have radical personal responsibility you can have radical self love and acceptance - and that's where real, permanent change happens. The only thing I ever lamented about this kind of work was that I hadn't started it sooner in my life. Over the years I developed a business mantra and I have found it really works when I am stuck in self-doubt. It goes like this:

Cook. Heal. Eat. Repeat.
Every day I cook up adventures in my life and in my kitchen
Every day I heal another layer of my heart wound
Every day I eat well to nourish my mind, my body, my soul
Repeat. Repeat. Repeat.

KEY READER TAKEAWAYS
Forming a New Habit

This mantra made me feel like the D.I.V.A. woman I wanted to be - daily, inspired, verifiable, action-oriented. Oxytocin is a chemical known in layman's terms as the "love hormone," and since women have been known to be caretakers to anyone and everyone but ourselves, it's very rare that we create our own oxytocin. I encourage you to pick an oxytocin-inducing action (one of the 3 listed below) that will promote your overall well-being and push you to build confidence. Take a step you would not dream possible. Remember this is a practice. A new habit. The average person needs 66 days of consistent practice to form a new habit, but I'm here to assure you I have done this work and you can too.

1. Nutrition

Every time you sit down or rush out the door to eat, take time to give thanks for the food and choose with intention. Ask yourself: will what I eat boost my energy or make me sluggish? Is this fuel food or is it comfort food? Women require foods rich in magnesium, which in turn is rich in oxytocin! Incorporate some of those foods, like dark chocolate, avocados, bananas, or almonds, into your daily diet.

2. Hugging

Giving someone a massage, cuddling, or a simple hug leads to greater levels of oxytocin and makes us happier people. Hug yourself at least 5 times throughout the day. Do it in front of a mirror and say one nice thing to yourself while you do it.

3. Kindness

One act of kindness a day or giving 2-5 people throughout the day a smile can increase oxytocin levels and lead to improved mood feelings. How easy is this? There's no reason not to try this method.

Chapter 8

It Is Never Too Late

My very first masterclass was called "Peeling the Onion" where I offered a space for people to come unpack their grief. It was not in a classroom or a workshop setting, it was a pure communal gathering. It was friendship around tables; three tables to be exact. I offered food, games, and space for conversation. I kept it lighthearted and fun, and encouraged people to get up out of their chairs, interact with one another, and try something new. The focus of this class was cooking with a partner, some of whom were total strangers, as I offered guidance and advice. I felt like the tour guide of the kitchen instead of an iron chef that was focused on perfection. I let myself and my students explore, get messy, and most importantly, I let myself and everyone else have fun. I repeated one of my favorite quotes for the class as we neared the end of the masterclass. I had borrowed it from my favorite chef, Rachel Ray.

"If you love it, if you appreciate it, and if you feel a connection with your creation, it will taste delicious!" I couldn't help but display a huge smile on my face while the words left my mouth. I truly believed this to be true and I hoped my students could see the value in it as well.

One of the biggest lessons I learned from starting my second chapter of life was that age is truly just a number. As cheesy as it sounds, it's true.

So what if I took years to find what makes me happy? Who cares if I was almost 70 by the time I found my passion? In hindsight I could see that I didn't have the necessary support system to make better decisions when I was younger. If I did, who knows how different my life would have looked. What I came to learn as I neared 70 years of life was that community is *essential* to success. We are not meant to face things alone; humans are not naturally solitary creatures. Of course solace and alone time is important from time to time, but you can't conquer all that life can and will be by yourself. That is a recipe for failure. It is crucial to find people who make you feel safe, people who lift you up and encourage your success, and people who don't expect perfection from you.

I made the idea of community one of the pillars of my business, and eventually clients started signing up to coach with me. I approached each session with one rule: be authentically you and I'll be authentically me. My clients loved my approach to sessions because while we were dealing with heavy and painful things, we also kept things fun and light. My business felt so opposite to that of the restaurant which was an entirely different environment filled with pressure and tension and stress. My work felt truly *fun* and I went through a second, unexpected divorce. I divorced myself from the notion that my money and my work had to feel hard and stressful - I could actually have fun and make money at the same time; it was incredible! After one of my very first one-on-one meals with a client, after I was done cleaning up champagne glasses and soaking up the work we had done together, I sat out on my patio and stared into the desert sky. I felt so proud of myself I could just jump up and down for joy. It was fun, it was therapeutic, and in my heart I felt truly accomplished and confident. I hadn't felt that way in a long, long time. I felt the urge to grab my journal:

At age 60 I discovered I had wings to soar and fly
For years I struggled emotionally just to get by
My life on the outside looked fine and "keen"
But my heart at 60 was nowhere to be seen
My dad had passed, my business slipping away
My marriage now a pile of divorce paper hay
I decided no matter what, no matter how
The time to change & recreate me was NOW
So HONOR, shout, sing and say
The time has passed and it is unfolding today
Ladies of the Kitchen simply put, is an extension of me
My passion of cooking for all to heal and just "BE"
Join me & others you will come to trust
In community we'll discover
How the art of cooking deserves attention and just a pinch of "fuss"

Once I was done writing this poem I started thinking about all the times in my life when the simple act of writing was incredibly important and helpful. I was an avid journaler and kept each and every journal I had ever filled up. In the glow of my successful day, and feeling so far removed from the pain of my past, I decided to go up into my office and pull out some of those old journals. *It won't be so painful to read them now that you feel so much better, Maria, come on, you owe it to yourself to see how far you have come.* I felt inclined to include some of those entries here in the hopes that my words can help you in some way, the way they helped me.

January 28, 1995

I bought this journal today with my best friend Linda. I bought it with 2 purposes in mind: a) to capture my experiences b) to force myself to take a daily inventory of my life. Hopefully to build more gratitude and self-awareness into it.

This year brings me into my 9th year of sobriety with Vince and our 7th year as business owners of Picasso's Cafe. My daughter is 21 years of age and my son is 16. It seems I worry 90% of the time about Picsasso's or Vince. I seldom worry about whether my daughter will have another crazy boyfriend, or if my son will get into drugs or get a girl pregnant as most mothers in my position do. Instead I worry (a lot) about what employee will not come to work or be late? What if we do not make payroll? I seldom wake up in peace ....unless like now I am alone and far away from it all...

I guess I do create a lot of my own crises OR I just take everything with too much too heart. I want to change that but in some ways that is just ME. I wish sometimes $$$ was not so necessary in the world. I just want to be able to end each day in peace and know that God is thinking: "Wow, I am so proud of that girl."

July 1, 2001

So much has occurred in the last 3 years. Jeff, my brother in law, died. Jack, my father in law, died and Marissa got married. Today, I am ONE more time going through rehab with Vince. I am surprised I am not angry with him, just myself. I do not know if my "denial" of the situation occurred because I was so focused on the business of Picasso's, my lack of al-anon meetings, or what. I do now I am NOT mad at him. I am just so very very sad. He is right, you know. There are times I wish he did have lung cancer – I think I would have somehow felt more equipped to deal with that instead of this crazy, unexplainable disease.

September 7, 2002

The counselor has asked me to answer: What do you like about yourself?

Well here goes pen to paper... I think I am a pretty nice , fun and compassionate person. I believe I have decent values and try to be kind to most people I meet. I think of myself as a good wife and mom. I certainly have tried hard in both departments. I think lots of 'teacher qualities' have remained in me but I do find I am impatient.

I like my smile, my shoe size, my small hands and I can't stand my hips, my height and my 'thinning' hair. Sobriety has not been easy but it is such a special gift when things are progressing. It has had its trials. But, in a funky and strange way it has brought our family all together.

March 22, 2003

So in less than two months, Vince will have two years of sobriety. In less than 48 hours I will be a wife of 30 years. Both unbelievable feats as far as I am concerned. Re: sobriety round #2

This has NOT been fun at all. However, the sense of closeness I have for Vince is quite unique. I have a level of respect for him that I had not had in a while.

RE: marriage of 30 years. I see now how much has changed. Our 1st ten years I spend literally so much time worrying about winning the love of his family and getting past their anger. Somehow I blamed them all for not accepting me as a good daughter-in-law. We also had a lot of fights about the kids going to a Catholic School. IN the end we agreed and to this day so glad we did. They have participated in so much and done sports. Yup this round #2 with the demon of alcohol sure has taken a toll on all of us.

August 22, 2011

Just a few months back, I filed for divorce. I am overwhelmed right now. So much is going on around me: the impending death of my dad (he has severe bone cancer), my plans to leave the restaurant, and my daughter completing her divorce.

I try to convince myself to stay calm and be at peace. Having Jay as my sponsor and the fellowship of Al Anon has helped make life bearable and tolerable. Has all this been fun? Hell NO. Have I skated through this with grace? NOT always I regret. Has all this been worth it?....well this is what I DO know: my divorce has been a result of 'unacceptable behavior'. And of course being self righteous I want to put more blame on him.....it is what it is.

June 9th, 2012

So here I am. Almost at age sixty. In fear and in JOY. Fear of not having enough money and insecure. Joyful knowing that somehow, someway God has always taken care of me. Would he dump me now? I need to keep thinking this no matter what. So here are some I am sticking this note on my car dashboard: My God is Good. Abundance is mine for the Asking. Peace will come. Joy and serenity are mind for the asking. I am not sure how I know I must make the transition into single life with calm, dignity and grace. I must stick to what is my own court. What a journey I have had –some horrendous and horrific tales between my ex and I. Screaming matches, blackout, hurts etc Moments in time I choose never to share with my kids. Yet, I know we had good times there too. I will try to embrace that and move forward. I am so sad and disappointed. I am going to work on not crying so much. I think I will look up some good books and resources on the divorce process and grief.

Dec 30th, 2017

I feel so whole and better as I enter 2017. I accomplished so much this year. Warren and I are daily growing and learning so much in our second chapter of life. I surprise myself physically and spiritually. I know everything will come in time. I am so pleased to have my life unfolding calmly. Learning to let go of fear and failure is not easy for me.

September 13, 2018

Today I am optimistic. I am growing my residual business and I am enjoying being a Grandma to Bella. I believe with all my heart one day I will have a cooking club and my own entrepreneurial business. I WILL. I CAN. AND SO IT IS.....thank you, thank you , thank you!

October 4th, 2021

My business Ladies of the Kitchen is unfolding. I am filled with enthusiasm and ready to meet the challenges of life. I feel after meditating that I require to dance more and have levity. So I think I will start with a poem:

> *Dance with skip Maria ..and a hop*
> *It is then that perhaps my Joy will pop*
> *Dance and my heart will sing*
> *It is time you see, time for my power to ring.*
> *Join ME I say to one and ALL I meet*
> *Dance with me, no need to look at our feet!*
> *It is our soul that leads and shows us how to turn*
> *Together our job is simple — keep willing to dance and learn!*

Everything I have today has arrived through a journey of pain, tears (good and bad) physical ailments, family fights, business loss, marriage gone etc etc ...It took all these losses for me to arrive where? TO PEACE! TO SERENITY! TO JOY!

So today, as I look out my window and see the bougainvilleas with love and the desert clouds above ....I hold my hand over my heart. Thank you!

January 29, 2022

My vision board Masterclass party was a success. I had a full house and it felt so good to deliver all the material I had prepared. This all feels so good to help others and I am working on the belief that this is MY year. YES my time to be Maria!

July 22, 2022

I am not sure where I heard or read this but I had to write it down. It will remain on my desk for the remainder of the year: We come to love not by finding the perfect person BUT by learning to love an imperfect person perfectly

And so it is ...half the year has gone. Am I proud? Am I content? Am I pleased as to where I am going. I think the answer is a thumbs UP!

As I read all of these journal entries, curled up in my favorite chair with my favorite blanket, I felt immense love. I felt immense love for myself, for my experiences, and even for my past. I loved how much my past had taught me, and I loved that I was starting to teach from those experiences. I realized while I was reading that I had kind of fallen away from journaling even though I knew how important it was and I vowed to start doing it more.

In 2023 I turned 70 and started journaling more than ever before. I had a dream journal, an affirmation with intention journal , and my gratitude journal that included daily thoughts and ideas. When I started writing this book in January of 2024 I actually went back and read my journals from 2023 because it had been such a transformative year.

Affirmation Journal: July 9, 2023

It is safe to play, dance and work in ease in my kitchen as this is where I embrace and discover amazing ideas and healthy recipes

It is healthy to spend time outdoors in exercise and with friends ...this is time well-spent

I am magical at what I do. Each time I speak and give myself in true service to others, it returns 10-fold to me. The more I love my partner and our life. The more romance and gifts arrive to me

Gratitude Journal: August 20, 2023

We spent last evening inside because of Hurricane Hillary. According to all the experts, there will be NO hurricane (just expect lots of rain). This statement was based on the fact that there has been no such experience in our desert community for over 25 years.

Warren and I had varying opinions on how to prepare. In the end (NO sandbags!) Yup, I thought sandbags would be good.

Today, a water pump arrived. NOT sure how with all the non-stop rain. It is coming down pretty strong. But that pump saved our courtyard from overflowing.

Our new sofa arrived yesterday morning also. just before the storm began which was late afternoon. I want to work on my book. Maybe today is that day? NO, I think not. Just some ideas, maybe? So I must trust that my life as I know it to be will continue to unfold with joy and abundance whether I complete it or not. However, I feel it is a must or bust...Believe it ....so it is!

Dream Journal: September 6, 2023

So when I woke up this morning, I was a bit annoyed. My neck was stiff. I am annoyed because I am not losing more weight and I also had a dream about Vince! I am at my mom's house and I am watering the lawn. In the distance I see a good looking man with his younger brothers (friends) all on bicycle-carts. They are throwing generous portions of candy , in wrappers on the neighbors lawns as a good-will gesture.

He stops and we begin to talk. We are in the midst of a great conversation, when Vince shows up. Angry, he picks up one of the candies and shouts: "what the hell is going on here?" I remember saying " Vince, please leave us alone!" I am clearly single in this scene as I have wiped my hands, I have no ring and remember muttering under my breath, he is no longer my husband. I am so annoyed... Why am I dreaming this now???

Gratitude Journal: December 16, 2023

I came across a picture of my 1st trip to hawaii with Warren. It was my birthday present from him in 2013. In the picture are our names written in the sand on the shores of Mauna Lani Beach Nature Preserve. Looking at this picture I remember how I spent hours combing the surf and coral for the perfect shell to dot the "I" in my name Maria. I wanted to make a photo book of this memory for Warren. Why didn't I? That New year's was a dream come true. We made reservations at a small restaurant that had limited seating on the beach. They told us they had a few seats left but not an ocean view. Much to our surprise when we arrived a couple had canceled their reservations and because I told them I was a Christmas baby they offered me their table ....right on the sand, spectacular ocean view!

It was such a magical evening with a sweet couple from Switzerland offering to take our pic. I felt soo over the top! I welcomed the New Year with more enthusiasm than I had experienced in the past 3 years. I put the picture back in the journal .... What a marvel? An oddity. Is it possible that this evening in 2023 (10 years later) that I am still happy with that man that swept me off my feet when I cried with shame sharing my divorce journey. That man that still manages to make me feel over the top...Just like that night on the shores of Mauna Lani Beach. I welcome 2024.

As I transcribe these journal entries it is September 14th, 2024 and I am finally coming to the end of writing this book. My heart could explode with gratitude and pride knowing that I have finally told my story, and that there is a chance it could maybe help you work through your own pain, and perhaps start your own healing journey. I encourage you to journal as much as possible, especially in the beginning of the healing work, so you can come back when you have a better grasp on your life, when you have shed the shame and guilt that you do not deserve to carry, and when you know how worthy you truly are.

KEY READER TAKEAWAY

The Beauty of Journaling

One of my first sponsors in Al Anon told me, "We have no rules, but our suggestions and tools work if you are consistent and willing. Maria, a tool that I believe is an absolute must is journaling...write, write, and write some more."

I was stubborn from the get-go. I had spent so much of my career life prior to this moment doing just that –writing on chalkboards in the classroom, writing comments on my Senior Final Exam Essays, writing reports for Senior Reps and Loss Control as a Bilingual Translator , and you want me to write? I was furious. However, I knew that there was a truth in what she said. Many of the women in the rooms were slowly and even wonderfully releasing codependent habits and a lot of that was attributed to writing. So In the Spring of 1987, I began a consistent journey with journal workbooks. Almost 12 years later, during a tumultuous fight, prior to the 2nd rehab I experienced with my ex-husband, we began throwing things at one another. The main item we were throwing? Each other's journals ...It was not a pretty sight, tearing pages, throwing books in the trash , stepping on them .

I believe I lost at least 10 or more in the process. However, that did not stop me from continuing to journal and embrace the 2 lessons from that experience.

The words I took time to write on paper were very raw, authentic, heartfelt and truly how I felt in the moment, therefore, a reflection. And two? Once I revisited what I had written, I realized that my aching aspirations had saved me...those were my desires.

Desires had cheered me on. Desires had given me hope. Desires gave me the necessary emotional and spiritual energy to keep me going even after a disappointment.

One of the biggest things I learned through my healing journey, and continue to learn to this day, is to stop trying so hard to be perfect. I built a story in my early childhood: Try, try again and do it perfectly." Yet, never once did my parents or teachers say, "beat yourself up in the process." I learned in time that affirmations are a wonderful healing & transformation tool. However, for them to work one must be consistent in not only saying them out loud, but writing them down as well. Day after day write them in a journal, close your eyes and then repeat them again. Speak, write, and read it back with conviction.

Pick three affirmations from the list below that resonate with you. Commit to 45 days.

Then change them up for another set of three. Before you know it, you have completed 1 year of affirmations and are releasing PERFECTIONISM! And, you'll have an entire journal filled with affirmations to reflect and look back on the following year. Here are the options:

*My worth is not based on being number one

*I will give myself grace when I make mistakes

*I value learning more than being perfect and right

*I am enough just the way I am

*I embrace the lessons that come with imperfection

*Done is better than perfect

*I do my best and my best is enough

*I am proud of who I am becoming, even with all my imperfections

Final Reflections

I created this recipe as a result of arriving at a place in life where my emotions, intellect, heart and mind have blended together to create the ONE and only "soul" ingredient I require daily. .....self love.

This book has been a vision of mine for over ten years. The loss of a business, a marriage and a parent simultaneously prompted me to believe someday my story may offer help and hope to another. So here is my special must have in the kitchen recipe I call Maria's Healing Harmony Seasoning:

May it bring it to your ears the crunch of joy
May it bring to your taste buds the sweetness of peace
May it bring to your sight a smile softness as it gently melts in your favorite AM beverage
May it bring to your smell the aroma of your favorite childhood sweet food
May it bring to your touch the ability to hug your soul wounds ; discover a healthy
harmony with your body.
May you savor its benefits.
Love, Maria

Healing Harmony Seasoning

Every ingredient you cook with holds a special energy. Just like when certain people walk into a room you automatically feel good. Herbs and plants have that same power/energy. In a spice it simply has been transmuted. So when you prepare each spice, think of its benefits, and the type of energy it brings to you.

You can use this seasoning anywhere that calls for pumpkin spice or a similar mix of spices when baking. It is also super tasty sprinkled onto sweet potatoes or your favorite hot latte or tea.

RECIPE

2 parts cinnamon —personal strength + clarity

1 part ground allspice— good fortune + healing

1 part ground ginger — romance, passion + power

1 part nutmeg—good fortune + intuition

**Make sure to purchase the best organic spices available to maintain their shelf life and energy. Store in a glass jar that is visible and add 2-3 cinnamon sticks. This wonderful seasoning will last up to three years at room temperature, but I am sure you will use it up in a heartbeat.

Made in the USA
Las Vegas, NV
17 November 2024